CONTENTS

STATEMENTS OF COMMITTEE MEMBERS

WITNESSES

QUESTIONS AND ANSWERS

SUBMISSIONS FOR THE RECORD

S. HRG. 109–522

HOSPITAL GROUP PURCHASING: ARE THE INDUSTRY'S REFORMS SUFFICIENT TO ENSURE COMPETITION?

HEARING

BEFORE THE

SUBCOMMITTEE ON ANTITRUST, COMPETITION POLICY AND CONSUMER RIGHTS

OF THE

COMMITTEE ON THE JUDICIARY
UNITED STATES SENATE

ONE HUNDRED NINTH CONGRESS

SECOND SESSION

MARCH 15, 2006

Serial No. J–109–65

Printed for the use of the Committee on the Judiciary

U.S. GOVERNMENT PRINTING OFFICE
28–340 PDF WASHINGTON : 2006

For sale by the Superintendent of Documents, U.S. Government Printing Office
Internet: bookstore.gpo.gov Phone: toll free (866) 512–1800; DC area (202) 512–1800
Fax: (202) 512–2250 Mail: Stop SSOP, Washington, DC 20402–0001

COMMITTEE ON THE JUDICIARY

ARLEN SPECTER, Pennsylvania, *Chairman*

ORRIN G. HATCH, Utah
CHARLES E. GRASSLEY, Iowa
JON KYL, Arizona
MIKE DEWINE, Ohio
JEFF SESSIONS, Alabama
LINDSEY O. GRAHAM, South Carolina
JOHN CORNYN, Texas
SAM BROWNBACK, Kansas
TOM COBURN, Oklahoma

PATRICK J. LEAHY, Vermont
EDWARD M. KENNEDY, Massachusetts
JOSEPH R. BIDEN, JR., Delaware
HERBERT KOHL, Wisconsin
DIANNE FEINSTEIN, California
RUSSELL D. FEINGOLD, Wisconsin
CHARLES E. SCHUMER, New York
RICHARD J. DURBIN, Illinois

MICHAEL O'NEILL, *Chief Counsel and Staff Director*
BRUCE A. COHEN, *Democratic Chief Counsel and Staff Director*

SUBCOMMITTEE ON ANTITRUST, COMPETITION POLICY AND CONSUMER RIGHTS

MIKE DEWINE, Ohio, *Chairman*

ARLEN SPECTER, Pennsylvania
ORRIN G. HATCH, Utah
CHARLES E. GRASSLEY, Iowa
LINDSEY O. GRAHAM, South Carolina
SAM BROWNBACK, Kansas

HERBERT KOHL, Wisconsin
PATRICK J. LEAHY, Vermont
JOSEPH R. BIDEN, JR., Delaware
RUSSELL D. FEINGOLD, Wisconsin
CHARLES E. SCHUMER, New York

PETER LEVITAS, *Majority Chief Counsel and Staff Director*
JEFFREY MILLER, *Democratic Chief Counsel*

HOSPITAL GROUP PURCHASING: ARE THE INDUSTRY'S REFORMS SUFFICIENT TO ENSURE COMPETITION?

WEDNESDAY, MARCH 15, 2006

U.S. SENATE,
SUBCOMMITTEE ON ANTITRUST, COMPETITION POLICY AND CONSUMER RIGHTS, OF THE COMMITTEE ON THE JUDICIARY,
Washington, DC.

The Subcommittee met, pursuant to notice, at 2:07 p.m., in room SD–226, Dirksen Senate Office Building, Hon. Mike DeWine, Chairman of the Subcommittee, presiding.

Present: Senators DeWine, Kohl and Schumer.

OPENING STATEMENT OF HON. MIKE DEWINE, A U.S. SENATOR FROM THE STATE OF OHIO

Chairman DEWINE. Good afternoon. We welcome all of you to the Antitrust Subcommittee hearing on hospital group purchasing organizations. This is the fourth hearing in the last few years that the Subcommittee has held on these organizations, known as GPOs.

I think it is fair to say that this is the most extensive investigation this Subcommittee has done, and I think to some of our friends in the industry it has felt much too extensive. But we have focused so much time and energy on it because of the importance of this industry to the health of our economy and, of course, to the health of our citizens.

The purpose of this hearing this afternoon is to evaluate where we stand today. Is this industry competitive or is legislation required to inject competition into the industry? As we have discussed before, GPOs are simply organizations that manage purchasing of medical equipment and supplies for most of our Nation's hospitals. Their ability to combine the purchasing power of the hospitals makes them an important part of the health care market.

Today, we will be evaluating current industry practices, as well as considering a number of legislative proposals for other ways that the industry could operate. I think a brief review of this Subcommittee's activity in this area will help to explain the various proposals.

We held our first hearing on GPOs in April 2002. We did it because of complaints of ethical violations in the industry and also a more general complaint that the GPO system sometimes decreased the flexibility of hospital purchasing and made it difficult for doctors and nurses to get the best medical equipment. We found, unfortunately, that both of these allegations had some merit.

During the course of our ongoing investigation, we also assessed a number of contracting practices, such as sole-source contracts, discounts based on high commitment levels, and bundling of clinical preference products with commodity products. All of these practices have positive aspects, but also may cause competitive difficulties.

Our analysis of the industry has been complicated further by the so-called safe harbor that underlies this industry. GPOs have an unusual business model. They are funded not by their member hospitals, but rather by their suppliers. In other words, GPOs agree to purchase equipment and supplies from certain companies and as part of those contracts, the suppliers pay an administrative fee based on the size of the contract which is used to fund the existence of the GPOs.

Under normal circumstances, this would be considered a kickback, and so the GPOs require an exemption from the anti-kickback laws. We have been told this safe harbor is what allows the GPO industry to exist in its current form. However, this relationship between the GPOs and the manufacturers have led many to distrust the purchasing decisions that GPOs make because, in effect, they benefit from larger contracts which are easier to sign with larger suppliers.

Despite the complexity of these issues, our efforts have paid off. Senator Kohl and I worked with the industry to resolve the ethical violations we uncovered. We also made some progress in assessing the various contracting practices and worked with individual GPOs as they agreed to adopt voluntary codes of conduct. And the good news is that the voluntary codes of conduct helped matters somewhat.

Smaller manufacturers seem to have greater access to the market, and the industry generally is more aware of the potential problems and has been taking steps to avoid additional problems. Under these circumstances, the Subcommittee has turned its focus to ensuring the permanence of the industry's reforms, and Senator Kohl and I introduced Senate bill 2880 last term as an effort to do that.

Senate bill 2880 would have given oversight of this industry to the Department of Health and Human Services, charging it with drafting rules for this industry to ensure that each GPO conformed with principles of competition, ethical standards and the goal of maintaining access to products necessary for proper patient care. If a GPO failed to follow these rules, it could lose its exemption from the safe harbor under that proposed legislation.

The GPO industry objected to this approach, and to address its concerns we agreed to hold off on introducing this legislation and allow them the opportunity to develop a method for ensuring their changes would be implemented effectively in a permanent way. The industry response is the so-called, quote, "Hospital Group Purchasing Industry Initiative," end of quote. This measure has been in place since July 2005, and it won't surprise our witnesses to hear some like it and some don't.

So today we are holding this hearing to consider whether the initiative has been effective at promoting competition in the industry, and we will consider what future steps, if any, are necessary to ensure that the reforms will be permanent and actively enforced. To this end, we will look not only at the effect of the initiative, but also at S. 2880, as well as two other proposals.

One of these proposals, which we are tentatively calling the individual code proposal, would empower Health and Human Services to codify and enforce the individual voluntary codes of conduct created by each specific GPO and set minimum standards for the codes. Another option is simply to repeal the safe harbor.

Now, before I turn to Senator Kohl, I would like to add that throughout this ongoing process I have kept in close contact with hospitals in my home State of Ohio, and I think it is fair to say that nearly all the hospitals in Ohio that I have spoken with are confident that their GPOs are saving them money. In this era of skyrocketing health care costs, this is obviously a very critical consideration and one that this Subcommittee understands very well.

Our goal has been and will continue to be to promote vigorous competition which will ensure that GPOs both save money and allow new and improved technologies to get to the market to help medical professionals better care for all of us. We must strike the right balance and we are committed to doing just that.

Let me now turn to Senator Kohl, who has taken a very active role in this issue.

Senator Kohl.

STATEMENT OF HON. HERBERT KOHL, A U.S. SENATOR FROM THE STATE OF WISCONSIN

Senator KOHL. Thanks very much, Mr. Chairman. Today, as you pointed out, we will consider what steps remain to be taken to ensure that competition prevails in hospital purchasing so that the abuses our Subcommittee uncovered in the last several years never return. We will need to carefully consider the industry's latest efforts at self-regulation. We will also examine possible legislative alternatives that we have drafted should the industry's efforts fall short.

The last year has witnessed important developments for all of us who care about competition in hospital purchasing. At the behest of our Subcommittee, the industry has created a new organization to set standards and monitor the purchasing activities of hospital group purchasing organizations. The purpose of this new industry initiative is to ensure that GPOs do not engage in anticompetitive or unethical practices that freeze out new and innovative medical device manufacturers from the hospital market.

The founders of this new industry initiative, the Nation's largest and most influential GPOs, are to be commended for voluntarily forming this organization. The goals of this organization and the goals of the work of this Subcommittee over the last 4 years are central to American health care, namely ensuring that physicians, patients and health care workers have access to the best and the safest medical devices, devices that can literally make the difference between life and death.

The final question that remains for us to consider is whether the organization is strong enough to do the job. The founders of the industry initiative now argue that the creation of this organization means that we need to do nothing more, that we can rely entirely on the initiative to guarantee an open and honest marketplace. They argue that any further legislation is not necessary.

In order to assess this claim, at least two vital questions must be answered. First, is this organization really up to monitoring what is taking place in this enormous multi-billion-dollar industry? And, second, does this voluntary industry initiative contain sufficient sanctions to prevent wrongdoing and to penalize those GPOs that violate its founding principles?

Any industry plan must include real and meaningful sanctions if any GPO violates ethical principles or the rules of free competition. In an industry as important to health and safety as the purchasing of medical equipment for critically ill patients, half-measures which do not assure that the best medical devices are available for patients are simply not acceptable.

We have legislative tools available should we conclude that the industry initiative falls short. In the last Congress, Senator DeWine and I introduced the Medical Device Competition Act. This legislation will give the Department of Health and Human Services the authority to forbid GPO business practices which are anticompetitive or unethical.

Other commentators have suggested an alternative approach, namely to forbid GPOs from receiving payments from hospital suppliers. Advocates of this approach argue that such a prohibition would remove an inherent conflict of interest in the present system. No longer would hospital vendors pay the very organizations that are supposed to negotiate with these vendors to get the best deal for their hospitals. We will therefore need to pay close attention to the testimony of our witnesses today as we evaluate whether we need to take any further steps.

Before closing, I must express my disappointment that no representatives of the GPO industry accepted our invitation to testify here today. GPOs' willingness to provide us with candid answers is a factor we will evaluate in determining whether self-regulation will suffice. We do thank the witnesses who are testifying for coming here today to testify, and we look forward to hearing their views.

Thank you, Mr. Chairman.

Chairman DEWINE. Thank you, Senator Kohl.

Let me just say that I am also sorry that we don't have any of the GPOs here today. After this hearing, I would like to announce that we will send them each a letter from the Subcommittee asking for their input about each of the proposals that we will be discussing today. We look forward to their input. I think their input is very, very important. We will invite them to give us that input and their point of view on that.

I have Senator Leahy's statement which I would ask at this point unanimous consent to make a part of the record, and it will be made a part of the record at this point.

We will now turn to our panel. Richard Bednar is senior counsel in the law firm of Crowell and Moring and he currently serves as the coordinator of the Healthcare Group Purchasing Industry Initiative. He is also the coordinator of the Defense Industry Initiative on Business Ethics and Conduct, and has served on the U.S. Sentencing Commission.

Mark Leahey is executive director for the Medical Device Manufacturers Association, the national trade association that represents over 200 manufacturers of medical devices, diagnostic products and health care information systems.

Prakash Sethi is University Distinguished Professor of Management and President of the International Center for Corporate Accountability at Baruch College, at the City University of New York.

Mina Ubbing is the President and CEO of Fairfield Medical Center, in Lancaster, in my home State of Ohio. She has been with the Fairfield Medical Center since 1979, serving in a number of roles, from internal auditor and accounting manager to currently serving as its CEO.

We welcome all of you, and let me turn now to our first witness, Mr. Bednar.

STATEMENT OF RICHARD J. BEDNAR, COORDINATOR, HEALTHCARE GROUP PURCHASING INDUSTRY INITIATIVE, WASHINGTON, D.C.

Mr. BEDNAR. Thank you, Mr. Chairman and Senator Kohl. Mr. Chairman, I think you have adequately summarized my current position with the law firm and with the industry associations that I work with as a coordinator.

I have been the coordinator of the Healthcare Group Purchasing Industry Initiative for 3 months, but I must add quickly that I have had well over 30 years of experience in working with other organizations in helping to develop organizational compliance and ethics programs. And I am very pleased to be with you today and to give you assurance that the Healthcare Group Purchasing Industry Initiative is off to a strong success.

The initiative was launched in May of 2005 by the CEOs of nine leading GPOs. The initiative is a permanent, all-voluntary, self-governing organization committed to the highest level of ethical conduct and providing the best and safest products to patients, doctors and health care workers at competitive prices. For brevity, I will refer to this initiative simply as the GPO initiative or the initiative.

The GPO initiative has three main purposes. First, it is intended to nurture and promote an ethical culture of compliance within every organization in the GPO industry. Second, the initiative promotes self-governance as the means by which each GPO's top-level commitment to abide by ethical standards is controlled. Third, the initiative enforces a requirement that each member of the organization share best practices in dealing with ethics and business conduct issues. This sharing of practices is done both informally by regular communication among the compliance officers as issues arise and by participating in an annual best practices forum.

To achieve these purposes, each GPO has pledged, first, to follow six core ethical principles; second, to report annually on adherence to these principles by responding to a public accountability questionnaire; and, third, to participate with other GPO representatives and interested parties in an annual best practices forum. The initiative is governed by a steering committee of the nine founding GPOs, who are, in effect, our board of directors.

Each signatory is required to follow six principles: first, to have and adhere to a written code of business conduct which establishes high ethical values and sound business practices; second, to conduct learning within the organization as to personal responsibilities under the code.

Third, each signatory is committed to work toward the goals of high-quality health care and cost-effectiveness. Fourth, each signatory is committed to work toward an open and competitive purchasing process, free of conflicts of interest and undue influence. Each signatory is responsible to each other to share best practices in implementing the principles, and each signatory, importantly, is accountable to the public.

The public accountability process requires that each member organization annually respond to a detailed questionnaire, which responses are displayed publicly on our website. And I must add that we have done that with the responses to the first annual questionnaire which were posted on our website for all to see a bare 2 months ago, and in that bare 2 months we have had over 26,000 visits to that website, to those postings, indicating a very strong public interest in what the GPO companies are about.

On January 11, 2006, the GPO initiative held its second steering Committee meeting. All nine of the founding GPO CEOs were there. I was there to witness it and I was there to see their enthusiasm and the energy that they manifested for this initiative. Then on January 12th and 13th, the initiative held its first best practices forum, about which I have described in greater detail for the record.

In the future, Congress can expect sustained, extensive transparency from the GPO initiative, and significant open debate about its practices. This self-governance process will work. The CEOs believe in ethical leadership as the best way to introduce ethical business conduct within their organizations. The CEOs do not believe in out-sourcing this responsibility. Already, participation in the initiative—

Chairman DEWINE. Mr. Bednar, could you close? We have a vote at three o'clock and we are going to lose this entire hearing, so everybody has 5 minutes.

Mr. BEDNAR. Thank you, Mr. Chairman. We do believe that the voluntary effort will serve the goals that have been articulated by this Committee and that no legislation is required. I look forward to your questions.

[The prepared statement of Mr. Bednar appears as a submission for the record.]

Chairman DEWINE. We appreciate it. Thank you very much, sir. Thank you. I thought you were getting close.

Mr. Leahey.

STATEMENT OF MARK B. LEAHEY, EXECUTIVE DIRECTOR, MEDICAL DEVICE MANUFACTURERS ASSOCIATION, WASHINGTON, D.C.

Mr. LEAHEY. Mr. Chairman, Senator Kohl, on behalf of the hundreds of innovative medical technology manufacturers MDMA represents, I want to thank you for your continued efforts to ensure that patients and caregivers have access to the best technologies at the best price. This industry is founded on physicians and engineers working together to enhance the quality of care. Unfortunately, patients and caregivers don't always have access to these products.

When this Subcommittee held its first hearing in October 2002, witnesses testified about troubling GPO practices, including but not limited to exclusive contracts, excessive fees and corporate conflicts of interest. At that time, we heard the GPOs say we can reform ourselves. Yet, today we find ourselves back in this hearing room for the fourth time in as many years.

And while I would like to testify that the GPOs have corrected their exclusionary practices, this is simply not the case. GPOs continue to bundle unrelated products and companies, execute long-term sole-source contracts, award no-bid contracts, collect excessive fees, and police the markets for the dominant suppliers in a way that excludes innovative, cost-effective technologies. And as a result, patients, caregivers and the American taxpayer are all suffering.

Now, despite the steadfast efforts of this Subcommittee, significant problems remain. Just last year, the Health and Human Services Inspector General looked at this very issue and the results were staggering. The IG found that six GPOs collected $2.3 billion in administrative fees from the vendors, and their operating expenses were a whopping $725 million.

These GPOs, I remind you, manufacture no product, nor do they distribute any product. You may ask where the rest of the money goes. Well, the GPOs would have you believe they return that back to their member hospitals. But the IG found otherwise. The IG found that GPOs siphoned off nearly $500 million for their own purposes, including for-profit business ventures. The IG also found that the hospitals receiving these funds—the majority of them did not reflect these admin fees in their cost reports to Medicare.

GAO reports and court evidence also challenge the premise that the GPOs are focused on getting the best products at the best price. And why would they, given the current fee structure? The more a hospital pays, the more money the GPO makes.

In addition to the fact that the current fee structure creates a disincentive to lower costs, it also provides select dominant suppliers the opportunity to buy exclusivity. In a recent antitrust case, it was shown that the president of a supply company met with a GPO executive in May of 2003 and this vendor executive stated that his company did $345 million in business with the GPO in the previous year and they paid the GPO $31 million in administrative fees. Now, that is nearly 9 percent, well above what the GPOs would have you believe they collect. And as an attorney said in the court case, when you tip the doorman that well, he is sure to keep folks out of the building. And unfortunately this is happening with the GPOs.

Documents in this case also showed that suppliers pay fees above and beyond the administrative fee. In fact, in a particular product category the dominant supplier paid the GPO 15.5 percent in fees for an exclusive contract for a sole source contract. However, if the markets were opened up and they needed to compete, the vendor was only willing to pay the GPO 4 percent in fees. This scenario is precisely why the GPOs are tempted to enter into exclusive contracts with dominant suppliers. They are prisoners to the fees. And, remember, the $31 million payment was from one vendor to one GPO for 1 year. Imagine what the impact is nationally to health care costs.

Now, GPOs claim that they can fix this problem among themselves, when evidence suggests otherwise. So long as the GPOs are allowed to sell restricted access to dominant suppliers by collecting payments from the largest vendors, patients, hospitals and taxpayers all lose out.

The GPOs will also claim that they need more time. Unfortunately, patients, caregivers and the American taxpayer don't have more time. But thankfully, Mr. Chairman, Senator Kohl, there is a solution. If you repeal the GPO safe harbor that Congress created nearly 20 years ago under much different circumstances, you will restore competition back in the marketplace and ensure that the GPOs are working for the best interests of their member hospitals and not the dominant suppliers who fund their activities. And if you do so, this will ensure that patients, caregivers and the American taxpayer suffer no longer and the future is much brighter for the health care system.

Thank you very much and I look forward to answering any questions you may have.

[The prepared statement of Mr. Leahey appears as a submission for the record.]

Chairman DEWINE. Mr. Leahey, thank you very much.

Professor, you are next.

STATEMENT OF S. PRAKASH SETHI, PROFESSOR OF MANAGEMENT, BARUCH COLLEGE, THE CITY UNIVERSITY OF NEW YORK, NEW YORK, NEW YORK

Mr. SETHI. Thank you, sir. For the record, I don't represent any industry or any interest group. I am here on my own behalf. I had to pay my own fare to come here.

Chairman DEWINE. Senator Kohl wouldn't pay for you?

Mr. SETHI. No. I asked them, actually. They said they had no budget, and it embarrassed my university when I asked them for the money to come here.

Anyway, I speak here only in my capacity as a university professor and president of the International Center for Corporate Accountability. This is a research organization based in the university and we do primarily work in the area of codes of conduct, how they are created, how they are managed, and essentially how they are implemented. I have spent a large part of my 30-year academic career on this work.

Before I talk about the GPO initiative, let me briefly offer you an overview of industry codes and discuss briefly the methodology we use at the ICCA for evaluating the substance, viability and efficacy of these codes.

Based on our research and field work in monitoring code compliance, we have identified eight conditions that must be met for an industry-made code to demonstrate measurable and credible compliance. Let me briefly summarize those eight points.

One, the code must be substantive in addressing broad areas of public concern pertaining to the industry's conduct. Two, code standards must be specific in addressing issues embodied in those principles. Three, the industry must create an independent governance structure that is not controlled by the executives of the member companies. And, four, there must be an independent external monitoring and compliance verification system, which is absolutely necessary to engender public trust and credibility in the industry's claims for performance.

Before addressing the GPO initiative, it is necessary to examine briefly the current GPO business model. Mr. Leahey mentioned something about that and so I do not need to repeat it. Based on our own analysis, it is evident that the current GPO model has built-in structure flaws and its financial incentives are so perverse that the GPO initiative cannot possibly remedy the situation.

We cannot talk seriously about a meaningful GPO initiative until Congress realigns the financial incentives so that the hospitals and not the vendors are once again the GPOs' only clients. As long as vendors continue to pay fees to the GPOs, any attempt to create, implement and enforce a voluntary code is doomed to failure. It would not improve the situation, but actually it would worsen it.

Let me now discuss the findings of our study of the GPO initiative. Over the last 6 months, my colleagues and I at ICCA have reviewed virtually all of the public records on the GPO issue and have evaluated the GPO initiative against the principles referenced above. This is the customary process and a necessary pre-condition for drawing objective and unbiased conclusions.

In my professional opinion, the six principles of the GPO initiative fail to measure up even at the very minimal level to any of the eight criteria we indicated. There is a total lack of independence in the initiative's governance structure, which is entirely controlled by the top executives of the member companies. Although the initiative includes a coordinator, the coordinator has no real authority.

The principles are essentially a statement of intent. All measures of substance are left entirely to the member companies. Industry members also set their own criteria with regard to compliance, performance evaluation, implementation assurance and public disclosure. Reduced to its bare essentials, the final product of this process becomes nothing more than a compilation of the reports provided by the member companies based on their own self-evaluation.

The governance structure of the GPO initiative does not provide any mechanism for independent external monitoring and verification of member companies' self-reported performance. Instead, it expects the public to accept this self-reported performance at face value. Such an assertion would be a dubious proposition under the best of circumstances. It would be untenable, given the industry's current record.

In summary, the GPO initiative is encumbered with a lack of specificity, non-existent performance standards and an internally controlled and self-serving governance structure, and an absence of genuine independent external monitoring. Furthermore, so long as GPOs continue to be funded by the vendors, meaningful and lasting reforms will not be possible because of the inherent conflict of interest that exists.

However, once this conflict is eliminated and all parties—namely hospitals, the GPOs and the suppliers—are actively committed to the principles and implementation conditions listed above, an industry code may prove a worthwhile exercise.

Thank you very much.

[The prepared statement of Mr. Sethi appears as a submission for the record.]

Chairman DEWINE. Professor, thank you very much.

Ms. Ubbing, thanks for joining us.

STATEMENT OF MINA UBBING, PRESIDENT AND CHIEF EXECUTIVE OFFICER, FAIRFIELD MEDICAL CENTER, LANCASTER, OHIO

Ms. UBBING. Thank you. I would like to thank Chairman DeWine and Ranking Member Kohl for inviting me to testify today. It is a special pleasure to be here before a fellow Ohioan, Chairman DeWine. I have some brief comments and would ask that my full written statements be put into the record.

Chairman DEWINE. They will be made a part of the record. Thank you.

Ms. UBBING. Thank you.

I am pleased to speak about the way in which the health care supply chain operates, having spent 27 years in the field of health care finance. In 2001, I was appointed president and CEO of Fairfield Medical Center, and before that served as Fairfield's CFO. We are a 222-bed hospital, not-for-profit, in a community, and we have become a major referral center serving the health care needs of southeastern Ohio.

I bring to this hearing my perspective not only as FMC's CEO, but also as Chair of a four-hospital Ohio Valley hospital consortium. I am also on the board of the Ohio Hospital Association, and in that sense I believe I speak for all 170 of that association's member hospitals and health systems.

As the members of this Subcommittee are undoubtedly aware, America's health care systems are under tremendous pressure to deliver health care at affordable prices and to do so without undermining the financial well-being of our delivery systems. In addition to providing top-flight health professionals, we must maintain an inventory of state-of-the-art technology, as well as goods and services, enabling us to provide the highest quality of care to every surgical patient, emergency room visitor, expectant mother and every individual seeking medical testing.

At Fairfield Medical Center, we purchase tens of thousands of goods and services, and have relationships with more than 1,600 vendors. While ours is a strong and well-respected hospital, we are relatively small and our power in the enormous health care purchasing marketplace is modest. That is why we have long been a member of health care group purchasing organization, or GPO.

For 22 years, FMC has been a proud member of Amerinet and we have reaped great benefits from that relationship by leveraging Amerinet's market expertise and power. The hard-dollar savings to FMC directly attributable to participating in Amerinet are roughly $1.1 million per year. These savings do not reflect the many other values that we get from being part of Amerinet, including education, assistance in negotiating for non-Amerinet products, and benchmarking FMC's performance against our peers.

Without the contracting services we get from our GPO, FMC would need to add at least five new professional purchasing staff at annual cost of some $400,000. Without the nationwide knowledge of products and prices our GPO maintains, we would be at a great disadvantage in negotiating our own contracts, which would further erode our pricing power.

Yet, not all our purchasing is through our GPO. To the contrary, only 63 percent of FMC's purchasing occurs through Amerinet. Of the top 500 items we purchase, only half come from GPO contracts. We buy the remainder directly from vendors. GPOs do not make purchasing decisions for hospitals. Rather, such decisions are driven by a variety of factors, including clinician preferences, our own comfort level with certain products and services, and the knowledge that our purchase is cost-effective, not just low-cost. Ultimately, if we are required to have it or if our clinical staff demands it, we try to purchase it at the best possible price. It is as simple as that.

One example of an item that our clinical staff required but we did not purchase through our GPO is a technology produced by a small Dublin, Ohio company that makes a gamma detection device used for cancer surgery. When we couldn't buy this item through our GPO, we went directly to the manufacturer and established a vendor relationship.

Sometimes, items can't be accessed through our GPO because the manufacturer will not sell to a GPO. This is often the case in items that are patented. It may be a legitimate new innovation and we will have to buy directly from the vendor.

That said, whenever we consider buying a new item, we rely on a wide array of resources to guide our decision, including input from clinicians, outside experts, manufacturers, consulting firms and our GPO. Fairfield Medical Center has a value analysis Committee to review all new technologies, whether they come to us at the request of a physician, through a trade show, or direct appeal from a vendor. Each prospective purchase is subjected to a 16-point value inspection to measure clinical benefit and cost-effectiveness.

The technological needs of our hospital are constantly changing. We can count on health care consumers to demand access to the best new technologies, just as our clinicians demand use of the same. We must be able to respond to these demands and that is why we have a system in place at FMC to identify and evaluate new medical technologies and to acquire them when doing so is the right clinical and financial decision for our hospital.

GPOs do provide immense value to FMC and other health care systems, even though they hardly control our purchasing decisions. The GPO model of charging administrative fees to suppliers and providing cost savings and other important benefits to FMC and its other members is critical for any health care system in today's economically challenging environment. This is particularly the case for small and rural systems like ours which have the least market power and the most to lose from margin pressures.

Over the nearly three decades I have been a hospital administrator, I have seen many unintended consequences of well-intentioned but misguided efforts to better control business practices in the health care sector. Where GPOs are concerned, I believe that any restrictive legislation would have a dangerous or ripple effect on America's hospitals—adverse consequences that would be felt more severely by small and rural systems such as ours.

I ask you to join me in recognizing the value GPOs bring to the hospital marketplace, and that, while important, these entities do not control the purchasing marketplace, but rather help to make it more robust, competitive and cost-effective in an informed environment.

[The prepared statement of Ms. Ubbing appears as a submission for the record.]

Chairman DEWINE. Thank you very much.

Senator Kohl.

Senator KOHL. Thanks a lot, Mr. Chairman.

Mr. Bednar, as the industry initiative coordinator, you know that we have said many times that for self-regulation to work it must contain meaningful sanctions for non-compliance, or in other words it must have real teeth. As I understand the industry initiative, the only sanction available if a GPO fails to live up to its obligations is the possibility of suspension by the steering committee of the industry initiative.

The steering committee, as you know, is made up of the CEOs of the GPO members of the initiative. So is the possibility of suspension really an adequate sanction to ensure compliance with the principles of the initiative? What would it really matter if a GPO was suspended from a private, voluntary organization such as this one? A hospital could still use the services of that GPO to buy products. So what difference would it make?

Mr. BEDNAR. Thank you, Senator Kohl. I think that is a good question to ask, and the answer is that there will be enormous peer pressure for conformance. This industry initiative is in perfect harmony with some of the best thinking about how organizations should govern themselves, and I refer specifically to the organizational sentencing guidelines, chapter 8. I refer to the rules of the New York Stock Exchange. I refer to the regulations of a number of Federal agencies that are involved in acquisition. All of those believe in the principle of self-governance as the best approach to assuring compliance and the development of an ethical culture.

Insofar as the sanctions are concerned, this initiative is not designed to tee up penalties for misconduct. It is designed to encourage ethical conduct. It is designed with the best interests of the industry involved, the health care industry.

I have witnessed the commitment and the sincerity of the CEOs who have formed the initiative and I believe that the initiative will soon grow. We have already attracted four additional GPOs even in the short period of time that I have been the coordinator. I think as the industry sees and perceives and understands the value that this initiative adds to the health care supply chain that others will try to emulate it, or will certainly emulate it.

Specifically, if a GPO does not comply with the ethical expectations to which it is committed, I think there will be enormous pressure on that particular organization to fall into line. That pressure will come not only from the other members of the GPO, but from me as well, as the person responsible for reviewing the responses. Also, I think it is important that all of the activities of the GPO are displayed for the public to see on a website. Transparency itself is a strong enforcement mechanism.

Senator KOHL. Dr. Sethi, in your view, is the sanction or the suspension of the industry initiative sufficient to ensure that GPOs comply with the principles, or is it really much too little?

Mr. SETHI. With all due respect, I don't think this initiative amounts to much, if anything. If you look at the six principles, it simply says thou shall be good, thou shall not lie. But they were supposed to do all those things in the first place. The fact that we are here and the initiative is here is because we wanted to, and they expected us to seek improvements.

But there is nothing in these principles or governance mechanism that provides any assurance that changes will take place. They are reporting what they want to report, not what we want to hear. There is no external monitoring mechanisms. Are they actually reporting what they are supposed to be reporting?

In an industry setting, best practices is an oxymoron because all they are doing is supporting each other so that nobody gets out of line. Where is an idea that there is a better practice and then we ask the industry whether or not it is complying with it? We have no specifics of what ethical standards they are talking about, we have no specifics about what type of report they would make, and we have no specifics about how do we know whether or not that report is accurate. I rest my case.

Senator KOHL. I will ask one more question and then we will turn it back to the Chairman.

Mr. Bednar, a key part of your job will be to address GPOs' compliance with the charter of the initiative. You will depend on information submitted to the initiative by the GPOs in response to a questionnaire to make the assessment. How will you verify that the information provided by the GPOs is accurate? Will there be any independent audit of the GPOs or will you rely entirely on the information that the GPOs supply to you?

Mr. BEDNAR. Thank you, Senator Kohl. My role as the coordinator for this initiative is comparable to the role I have held with the defense industry initiative; that is to say I am the coordinator of that initiative as well. By experience, it is very easy to tell the sincerity and the commitment of the responses to the annual questionnaire.

First of all, there is an instruction that the company has to be very detailed in preparing its responses. Second of all, the questions themselves are very penetrating. Third, the responses require documentation and reference to organizational supporting documents, policies and practices. Fourth, the responses are displayed publicly for all to see on our website and for all to judge on our website.

Finally, we have now planned in future best practices forums to invite in outsiders to participate with us in the annual best practices forums so that there will be additional witnessing of the sincerity and the commitment of this organization.

Senator KOHL. Well, we will come back to it, Mr. Chairman.

Chairman DEWINE. Thank you, Senator Kohl.

Ms. Ubbing, I was interested in your testimony about the fact that you purchase items outside the GPOs. Could you give us an estimate of what percentage of your purchases are outside the GPOs?

Ms. UBBING. Yes. All of our purchases outside the GPOs amount to about 37 percent of purchases; 63 percent are within the GPO.

Chairman DEWINE. And what would those generally be? Can you give us a—

Ms. UBBING. Outside the GPO?

Chairman DEWINE. Sure.

Ms. UBBING. It could be anything from sutures to technology. It could be information technology, as opposed to clinical devices. It could be a medication. It could be any type of purchase.

Chairman DEWINE. And why do you purchase outside the GPOs, then, in each one of those cases? I mean, in general, why?

Ms. UBBING. OK. Quite often, that is driven by clinical preference of our practitioners who are using the devices. Particularly with physicians, if they have been trained to use one type of a device and the GPO contract calls for another, it is their time and it is our risk as well as theirs for them to have to go into a procedure with equipment that they are not comfortable with.

Another reason is availability of connectivity. Take IV pumps. If all our IV tubing has come from one company and the contract with the IV pumps is from another, the conversion and the cost to our organization would be huge to have to change things that aren't broken to replace something that we want to update.

Chairman DEWINE. Would you say that Fairfield Medical Center is typical in that sense? Do you think most hospitals would be about one-third outside?

Ms. UBBING. I would think so, sir. I am not absolutely positive of that. I do not have data to support that, but certainly I know other hospitals go outside. And particularly your children's hospitals and some of those hospitals would have to go outside simply because the products are not in the contracts.

Chairman DEWINE. Mr. Leahey, why wouldn't Ms. Ubbing's testimony refute your argument? The hospitals are exercising judgment. They can go out and find other innovative products.

Mr. LEAHEY. Again, I think if you look at the market power of the GPOs, $80 billion or whatever it is they bring through, they are the gatekeeper. And while there may be a small percentage—

Chairman DEWINE. Her testimony is they are not the gatekeeper for her. She would say that, look, when we see a product and our doctors say we want a product, she goes out and buys the product, if their internally is need for the product.

Mr. LEAHEY. With Amerinet, I have one of their contracts in front of me here and they do allow a supplier to sell directly to the hospital, but it is interesting that Amerinet requires a waiver in order for this to happen. You would think that if it was really in the best interests of the hospital, the vendor should sell directly to them without needing a waiver from Amerinet.

And again when you look at the market-leading GPOs—Novation, Premier and others—they have tremendous influence in the marketplace and they do not always permit other products to get to the market.

Chairman DEWINE. Well, I am still trying to understand. Of course, this is not the first panel we have heard from and we have heard from other panels who have told us that—other witnesses have told us that innovation has been stifled and we have had some pretty strong testimony in this area. So this is the background, but as far as just the testimony we are hearing today, Ms. Ubbing is telling us that at least in her hospital she has been able to exercise the ability to go outside the contract. She doesn't seem to be too stifled by it.

Mr. LEAHEY. Well, again I could give you dozens, as I have for the staff as well—dozens of companies who are still excluded from the marketplace. One, in particular, here that I think is very important—this is a syringe; I don't know if you see it. It has a needle at the top. When you press the plunger, the needle goes in; there are no needle sticks. It saves caregivers lives here. They are offering this at 10 cents a syringe to Premier hospitals. The competitive product is about 28 cents. This is still getting locked out of the market.

And when you talk and you read about some of the company's call sheets, they say that Premier didn't let their hospitals know about this. And why would they, when the GPO model incentivizes them to do otherwise? They make more money the higher the price of the product. It is not in their best interest currently to allow for the better product at a cheaper price to enter the market.

So I think, you know, there are real problems here that we need to address. And, you know, some of the issues about the cost of bringing new staff in—5 new staff, $400,000—we are not saying the GPO model needs to go away. Any efficiencies that currently exist in the market will still exist and the providers and suppliers will still enjoy those. We are simply saying modify the revenue stream, realign the incentives of the GPOs so that they get the best products at the best price for their hospitals and aren't worried about policing the market for their dominant suppliers.

Ms. UBBING. May I comment?

Chairman DEWINE. Sure.

Ms. UBBING. With respect to an item like Mr. Leahey has shown, in our organization we actually had a vendor fare to look at the different devices that would protect our health care workers from needle sticks. As a result of that, the GPO was not the gatekeeper of what vendors came forward for us. We make those decisions. We are not bound by a contract with the GPOs not to look elsewhere.

Chairman DEWINE. Could one make the argument that if a hospital was not as aggressive as your hospital that it would be certainly easier to go with whatever the GPO had?

Ms. UBBING. I don't think so. We have got too many cost constraints and too many problems to do that. In fact, when we work with our GPOs, quite often we ask them to go look at different product brands on our behalf and we name the product brands.

Chairman DEWINE. Ms. Ubbing, let me ask you another question. I don't really quite understand the economics of this and maybe you can help me with it. You have stated that if you were to repeal the safe harbor and hospitals had to pay for GPOs directly, costs would go up. I don't quite understand that. Do you want to explain that to me?

Ms. UBBING. Certainly.

Chairman DEWINE. I mean, it seems to me that a cost is a cost is a cost. I mean, somebody is going to pay for it.

Ms. UBBING. And I think that exactly comes into play, but I think the reality is if the GPOs incur expenses, incur other activity opportunities that are no longer paid for by the vendors, those costs are going to invariably get back to the hospital. Consequently, those may or may not be allowable costs for us on our cost report. Therefore, you are going to lose reimbursement from your Medicare and Medicaid payers. Ultimately, we will lose in terms of items and services that we are allowed to get through our GPOs, particularly on the services side.

Chairman DEWINE. So what you are telling me is that this is a Federal reimbursement issue, actually.

Ms. UBBING. It has the potential to be. Our Federal reimbursement is capped, as you know, by the Medicare DRG system, prospective payment system. And at the same time, vendors are not capped from what they charge us. Certainly, we can enter into a GPO contract that for a period of time we will retain a price. But anything that is new or anything that is innovative that we want to go to, drug-eluding stents being a classic example of this, the Medicare provisions did not initially allow—when drug-eluding stents were finally approved, did not allow an increase in our reimbursement for the use of those, and the difference in price was significant.

Chairman DEWINE. Mr. Leahey.

Mr. LEAHEY. Mr. Chairman, if I may, again I think it is—

Chairman DEWINE. Let me just say we have two other witnesses here. Anytime you two want to jump in, don't be bashful. You know, this is kind of like "Hardball." The only way you are going to get in is just jump right in. Or "Crossfire" maybe is a better thing, so you just jump in.

Mr. LEAHEY. This absolutely is a cost issue and a Medicare reimbursement issue. Again, I think as the HHS IG pointed out, when you have many hospitals not reflecting this in their cost reports, there is an issue here. And I think it is fantasy to think that somehow these GPO fees are free money. No supplier is going to absorb these costs.

Chairman DEWINE. Well, somebody is paying for it.

Mr. LEAHEY. Absolutely, and there is a margin that needs to be made. So if the companies have to pay the GPO on the top, they have to pass the costs on to ultimately the customer or the hospital, or more importantly Medicare, who pays 46 cents on every dollar.

Chairman DEWINE. Ms. Ubbing, this controversy just keeps going on and on and on, and the critics of this system keep beating you all over the head with it. I mean, sometimes you just want to take an issue off the table. It seems to me that just paying out for a service is sort of the American way, isn't it? I mean, paying directly for a service is sort of what we do everyday. If I want to buy something, I pay for it. This kind of back-door payment is not really the way we usually do things in this country, is it?

Ms. UBBING. I think I would draw an analogy for you of this: If I have the opportunity as a hospital to buy at a Sam's Club or someplace where the items have been bought in bulk and I can take advantage of the same pricing that a larger hospital or a larger system could also get because of the volume involved there, that is great. If I have to go out one-on-one and negotiate a price, and the price is going to be different—I know this from ongoing activities—from hospital to the next, that is putting a lot of burden on me and is not lowering the cost of health care.

Chairman DEWINE. Sam's Club does have a membership fee, I think.

Senator Schumer.

STATEMENT OF HON. CHARLES E. SCHUMER, A U.S. SENATOR FROM THE STATE OF NEW YORK

Senator SCHUMER. Thank you, and I am sitting here and I am burning up. Here we have industry people who are making record profits. We have most of our hospitals in New York losing money. They try to get together and form an organization that will save them money and give them some bargaining power and they end up looking like the bad guys. This is ridiculous.

Why would hospitals want to pay more money? They don't. I know hospital executives throughout New York. Most of them are non-profit and they have to lay off people everyday and they have to cut back services everyday. One of the few things they can do, as Ms. Ubbing said, is band together so they might have some bargaining power because they don't have the ability like a company to hire 20 salesmen and go knock on doors and sell their product. And we want to not let them do that?

There may have been abuses in these GPOs, but I will tell you something. I sure as heck don't want to see them eliminated, paralyzed, handcuffed so that some businesses can make even more money. This is getting to the point of absurdity here, to the point of absurdity.

We have the same thing with hospital reimbursement rates. In New York, we have got 25 percent of our hospitals close to bankrupt because the insurance companies have the bargaining power, because there are 30 different hospitals and only 4 or 5 different providers and we are not getting the health care we need.

The idea that hospitals, Mr. Leahey, would want to pay more for an item, unless something is crooked, makes no sense. And the idea that ten of them can bargain with you instead of one-on-one bargaining with you is a good idea, not a bad idea, and it will bring your price down on your thing from 10 cents to 8 cents. You may not want that, but I want that, Medicare wants that, Medicaid wants that, the Government wants that and the consumer wants that.

So I mean I didn't come in here intending to make such a fuss, but as I sit here—it is not my way, of course.

[Laughter.]

Senator SCHUMER. But as I sit here, you know, sometimes governments take an excess, which there was, and then they throw out the baby with the bath water. And for the next 10 years we are underwater, suffering, and that is what I fear is happening here.

I have looked into this a little bit. I have seen that the GPOs are really now making an effort to self-police and bring down costs, and it is in their interests. I just spoke with the head of a—not on this issue, but with the head of a major New York hospital 2 hours ago, a huge system, and he is a decent person. I have known him for 25 years. He is agonizing about what to cut. He is agonizing about who to lay off, after they have had such pride in all this. He is not going to play a game and pay 28 cents for an item that he can get for 10 cents.

And the theory of GPOs makes sense and we ought to make sure that the actuality makes sense, and I think most of the time it does. The purchasing initiative that they have, I think, a large number of hospitals are participating in, and again it is just common sense. A company that makes syringes will have its only mission to sell as many syringes as it can at the best price it can. That is your job. But a hospital can't equal that energy for every product in every area and do as good a job. So the idea of people coming together and saying let's find one expert to buy syringes for all the hospitals in Ohio or New York or somewhere else and bring the price down is what makes sense.

You know, we didn't do that in the Medicare bill. We didn't allow Medicare to bargain with the pharmaceutical industry. Guess who was happy? The pharmaceutical industry. Guess who lost out? A lady I just spoke to in Buffalo who can't afford a cancer drug. Her $2,000 is up. She will never get past the donut hole because she won't pay $5,000. She is in agony, she is in pain.

Chairman DEWINE. Senator, let me—

Senator SCHUMER. I am sorry.

Chairman DEWINE. I have an advantage over you. I can see the screen and I know a vote just started. That is the only advantage I have.

Senator SCHUMER. I am sorry. But, anyway, I just hope we don't take this too far. That is all.

Chairman DEWINE. Well, we are not going to take it too far, and let me just say neither Senator Kohl—I don't speak for Senator Kohl, but neither Senator Kohl nor I have any intention—no one is talking about doing away with these at all. You know, the question is how it is fine-tuned and how we move from here.

Senator Kohl.

Senator KOHL. Right. We are not talking about trying to do away with GPOs. They are a good thing and we want to ensure that they operate in a most effective and fair way. I mean, that is the point.

Some of our concern, Senator Schumer, is that the GPO sets up its organization and then hires a person whom they pay and whom they can fire to be the administrative executive of that organization. You know, we are here to look at things and look at the surface and look behind the surface, and finally as a result of all the work we have done we would like to set up something that polices itself, but really gets the job done effectively.

Senator SCHUMER. Well, I am for that.

Senator KOHL. And you don't disagree with that.

Senator SCHUMER. I agree with that.

Senator KOHL. None of us disagrees with that.

My own personal concern is not that you are not a fine person. That is not the issue. They hire you, they can fire you, and you are going to be a part-time administrator. To us, having put in all this work and all this time and all this effort—we don't know anything about you as a person; you may be great. But in my own mind, I am concerned about this initiative coming to us and saying you can now, Congress, go away because we are setting up this organization and we are going to hire the executor and we are going to police him and then we will fire him for any reason we want. That, to me, doesn't sound like the kind of oversight that we have been trying to organize and get settled.

But I have said my piece and perhaps you want to talk.

Mr. BEDNAR. Well, with all due respect, Senator—

Chairman DEWINE. OK. Now, we are going to give you 30 seconds and we are going to give Mr. Leahey 30 seconds.

Senator SCHUMER. The Chairman just asked him to say something a few minutes ago. Now, he is.

Chairman DEWINE. No, no, no. Here is the problem. We have a vote now and this is going to end, so we are going to be out of time.

Mr. BEDNAR. We believe the initiative has picked up exactly in the way that this Committee had advised the industry to pick up. And I am only a small player in this; I am just the coordinator, the executive director, if you will. The real energy and the real commitment comes from these nine CEOs who formed this initiative and they are the ones who are responsible for setting the tone from the top in a way that I think will eventually prove to be very, very successful. Give us time to prove that to you.

Chairman DEWINE. Mr. Leahey.

Mr. LEAHEY. Thank you, Mr. Chairman. Well, this is the fourth hearing in as many years, and again we understand there is a potential value in the GPO model. We are not against hospitals aggregating their volume. And again our members are not the J&Js, the Medtronics, the Guidants. They are the little guys who are innovating products at a better price.

Aggregating volume absolutely makes sense. We are not against that. The problem we have here is the funding mechanism. The hospitals aren't looking to contract for more expensive products either. The problem is the GPOs, who are the middlemen—there is the perverse incentive in place. They are the ones who are receiving more money the higher the price of the product is. So I don't think this is a hospital issue.

So long as the GPOs are funded by the vendors whose products they are charged with independently evaluating on a cost-plus model, this is not going to provide the Medicare system savings. I think that is exactly why the Department of Justice has an ongoing criminal investigation into these issues about Medicare fraud.

Chairman DEWINE. We are going to submit to all of you some written questions. One of the written questions will be for your comment about all the four proposals. I wish we had the opportunity to do this in open session and listen to your comments. We would appreciate you all getting back to us in writing.

Also, this Subcommittee has received letters on this issue from a variety of interested members of industry, including eight from Ohio—the Ohio Hospital Association, Mercy Children's Hospital, Lima Memorial Hospital, Akron General Health System, MedCentral Health System, Upper Valley Medical Center, Ohio Children's Hospital Association, Catholic Health Care—and several other letters as well. We will put all of these in the record.

Any additional comments? My colleague from New York.

Senator SCHUMER. I will be very quick. I heard you read a list of hospitals in Ohio. I have hospitals in New York. I mean, they are not dumb. They sort of know what they are doing and they know they have to lower costs. So I would need a lot of evidence to show that the GPO, which is sort of set up and run by the hospitals, isn't doing what is good for the hospitals. Now, if that is the case, we ought to change it, no question about it.

But it seems to me the hospitals, which are sweating every minute over every nickel, at least in New York, would have a pretty good idea if they are getting rooked. And they wouldn't be so much for these organizations if they are as bad as some people are saying.

Chairman DEWINE. Well, I would just point out to my colleague that because of what this Subcommittee has done, we have made some substantial changes. And I don't think there are too many people in the room who don't think we have made some substantial changes.

Senator SCHUMER. Mr. Chairman, I agree with that.

Chairman DEWINE. We have come a long way.

Senator SCHUMER. I just think what seems to be happening now with all the new awareness, the self-policing—they are much tougher on it—seems to be working. And I just sort of smell out there that at least there are some people who would want to make the GPOs unworkable, not on this Committee, obviously, but some people who would think they would do a better job without the GPOs bargaining with each hospital.

Well, we want to thank all the members of the panel who have come in. We appreciate it very much. We know you have taken your time and in some cases your money to get here, and we appreciate all of you being here. Thank you very much. It has been very helpful.

[Whereupon, at 3:10 p.m., the Subcommittee was adjourned.]

[Questions and answers and submissions for the record follow.]

QUESTIONS AND ANSWERS

Senator DeWine's Written Follow-up Questions:

1. There are nine GPOs represented by the initiative, and many others in the market as well. By any standard, that is a lot of competitors. Are there not enough GPOs out there competing with each other to keep them working to create value for hospitals? If not, and if GPOs do not effectively lower costs and prices for their member hospitals, why don't we see more hospitals leaving them, switching to other GPOs, or otherwise forcing them to improve?

Intensity of competition depends on a number of factors where the number of competitors is only one such factor. Companies' response to the marketplace ranges all the way from intense competition to substantial cooperation among potential competitors. This would be based on rational decision-making and does not have to involve intentional complicity or illegal conduct.

We must remember that companies compete only when they feel that they have a competitive advantage in terms of better product, service quality, or other aspects of buyer-supplier relationship, which would help them (a) gain market share from the competitors, and (b) earn greater revenues and extra profits. Therefore, it stands to reason that companies would not be inclined to compete – and just as likely to cooperate or even collude - when they see greater profits in competition avoidance. This would be true even where there is no direct collusion or cooperation. Collusion, under these circumstances, is more likely to happen where the rewards of collusion far exceed potential risks of discovery and punishment.

The fact that nine GPOs are part of the HGPI Initiative does not make the system more competitive. The GPO industry has argued that there are more than 600 GPOs and also that more that 30 GPOs are engaged in some level of nationwide contracting. We can effectively demonstrate that current GPO industry structure is largely anti-competitive and would remain so given the current industry structure and operating procedures. This can be seen both on the basis of economic theory and factual data from the GPO marketplace.

The present day GPO organizations have the following characteristics all of which serve to discourage intra-industry competition:

1. They are a classic case of an oligopolistic industry where top 2-3 players control more than 70% of the industry's sales, and largely set the standard of conduct for other players. The current industry structure, i.e., domination by 2-3 companies has been the result of industry-wide consolidation that took place during the late 1980s and early 1990s.

   This consolidation was the logic step for the major players to take because the universe of the hospitals is finite and, with few exceptions, a vast majority of these hospitals had already been signed up by a GPO. The large GPOs can therefore capture extra profits by buying out the smaller ones, which either compete or have the potential of competing with the larger GPOs. Given market saturation, additional revenues can be generated only through consolidation and capturing revenue streams of the acquired companies. Smaller companies find it attractive to sell because of the premium price offered by the larger players, who can easily pass on the extra costs to the customers through increases in their operating costs. The only GPOs left out from these combinations are likely to be the ones that provide specialized services or serve remote areas that cannot be served more effectively by the larger GPOs.

   The current larger GPOs have no incentive to compete with each other. They provide essentially similar services and draw from the same pool of suppliers. Profits would, therefore, come not from greater efficiencies but increased monopoly power. Unfortunately, this is not possible since the current GPOs are already quite large and any additional consolidation would attract regulatory inquiries.

   There is another equally important reason for the large GPOs not to compete with each other. Given the fact that their target of competition is another equally large GPO, the potential competitor would offer strong resistance to losing market share. Therefore, the end result of such competition is more likely to result increased costs to the two players. There is also the added risk to unintended disclosure of market practices of the GPOs which may not be looked upon favorably by their customers, i.e., hospitals or the regulators seeking lower costs and greater efficiencies from the GPOs.

The result of such a competitive landscape is that the top 2-3 companies adopt a posture of "live and let live."

2. The current pattern of cooperation, or competition avoidance, is also facilitated by high entry barriers that deter outsiders to seek entry into the GPO market either as new start ups or by buying an existing GPO. It is prohibitively expensive for a new entrant to gain significant market share because most current and potential customers are already locked in through various contractual arrangements.

3. Unlike the GPOs, hospitals are currently poorly equipped to undertake effective cost/benefit analysis. For them to be able to do so, we must find a way to provide them with the resources that are currently available to GPOs through the safe harbor and the 3% administrative fee. I have made a recommendation in this direction in my response to the three proposals that the three options before your Subcommittee.

2. Senator Kohl and I have provided each of you with four proposals for ensuring that the GPO industry and markets for medical devices function as effectively as possible.

Option 1 is to reintroduce S. 2880, the bill that we introduced last term. This bill gives the Department of Health and Human Services the ability to enact rules that spell out what kinds of conduct are contrary to ethics and competition principles. HHS would then certify that each GPO is avoiding such conduct under its rules, and if a GPO fails to be certified, it would lose the safe harbor.

Option 2, which we are calling the "voluntary codes option," would give HHS oversight to determine whether the GPOs are each complying with their own individual codes of conduct. HHS would require minimum standards for the individual codes of conduct, and, like S. 2880, HHS would then certify each GPO under its rules; if a GPO does not get certified, it would lose the safe harbor. In addition, the antitrust agencies would be able to provide input as to whether each GPO gets certified.

Option 3 is, simply, repeal of the safe harbor.

My detailed responses to the three options are attached.

Finally, Option 4 is that we could rely on the Industry Initiative as it is currently constructed.

Please discuss your opinions of each of these proposals.

As I indicated in my March 15 testimony before the Subcommittee, I do not believe we can rely on the Industry Initiative to correct the U.S. healthcare purchasing system.

My analysis strongly suggests that the current modus operandi of GPOs, doing business under the protection of the Medicare anti-kickback safe harbor, has contributed to a misallocation of a very large portion of the revenue received from vendors in the form of fees and other considerations. Regrettably, the failure of the industry members to address the questionable practices revealed by the Subcommittees in the nearly four years -- since this panel first urged them to institute a code to police themselves -- continues the pattern of resistance to change that we have seen time and again with industry codes.

In my professional opinion, the current GPO business model and legal framework has built-in structural flaws, and its financial incentives are so perverse that the GPO Initiative cannot possibly remedy this situation. Anti-competitive contractual arrangements, industry concentration, and especially the vendor-financed fee structure -- all of which arise from the Medicare anti-kickback safe harbor -- have created strong incentives for the GPOs to maximize their income, and equally strong disincentives to distribute this income to their beneficial owners, i.e. hospitals and nursing homes. Indeed, the structure of the new GPO Initiative seems to indicate that its entire purpose is to protect the industry's anti-competitive exclusionary system in which the GPOs' self-interest takes precedence over the welfare of the industry's clients, including healthcare providers, taxpayers, and potential new entrants in the industry.

I do not believe that we can even begin to talk seriously about a GPO Initiative until we have realigned these financial incentives so that the hospitals, and not the vendors, are once again the GPOs' only clients. As long as vendors continue to pay fees to the GPOs, any attempt to create, implement and enforce a code of conduct is doomed to failure.

Even a cursory reading of the six principles contained in the GPO Initiative would make it obvious that they urge the member companies to do things that they should have been doing in the first place. What is missing, and what is needed, is an honest recognition of the member companies' activities that have been found to be inappropriate and a commitment to meaningful and verifiable reform. Among the most serious shortcomings of this Initiative are:

1. There is a total lack of independence in the Initiative's governance structure, which is entirely controlled by the top executives of the member companies. Although the Initiative includes a "coordinator," the coordinator has no real authority.

2. Principles are essentially a statement of intent. Any description of what these principles might contain by way of substance is left entirely to the member companies.
3. Member companies also set their own criteria with regard to standards of compliance, performance evaluation, implementation assurance, and public disclosure. Reduced to its bare essentials, the final product of this process becomes nothing more than a compilation of the reports provided by the member companies based on their own self-evaluation.
4. The governance structure of the GPO Initiative does not provide any mechanism for independent external monitoring and verification of member companies' self-reported performance. Instead, it expects the public to accept this self-reported performance at face value. Such an assertion would be a dubious proposition under the best of circumstances. It would be untenable given the industry's current record.

The new GPO Initiative is encumbered with a lack of specificity, non-existent performance standards, an internally controlled and self-serving governance structure, and an absence of independent external monitoring system. It is unlikely to yield any meaningful reform. Instead it would exacerbate the problem through absence of meaningful change and would further erode the credibility of its sponsors.

It is unrealistic to expect an industry to create a viable code or initiative that has been operating with a business model based on perverse financial incentives, a questionable legal structure, and federal statutes that undermine the imperatives of competitive markets. Therefore, the repeal of the safe harbor must precede any discussion of a GPO industry code of conduct or initiative.

Senator Sessions's written follow-up questions:

1. In your testimony, you made the serious allegation that hospital group purchasing organizations (GPOs) have engaged in illegal activity. Please provide the Committee with information regarding the nature of the illegal activity and any statutes violated.

My comments were based on media reports on the various investigations now being conducted into GPO activities by the Department of Justice, the Inspector General of the Department of Health and Human Services, and the Connecticut Attorney General, and various civil antitrust lawsuits.

Senator Kohl's Written Follow-up Questions:

1. Do you believe that the GPO Industry Initiative contains sufficient oversight over the functioning of GPOs, or is it too dependent on industry self-reporting?

GPO Industry Initiative has no effective independent oversight. The entire process is designed to generate information where the content is totally controlled by the industry members. The coordinator is not an independent evaluator and reports to the Steering Committee, which is composed of the CEOs of the companies whose performance is being monitored and evaluated.

In any detailed and objective analysis of the Initiative, it would become clear that the Initiative's six principles are not designed to generate information that would reveal conflict of interests on the part of GPOs. Nor do they specify any clear cut, objective, and measurable standards against which the performance of GPOs would be measured.

In my extensive experience working with corporate and industry codes of conduct all over the world, I have identified eight conditions that must be met for an industry-based code to demonstrate measurable and credible compliance with the industry's voluntary initiative.

1. The code must be substantive in addressing broad areas of public concern pertaining to industry's conduct.
2. Code principles or standards must be specific in addressing issues embodied in those principles.
3. Code performance standards must be realistic in the context of industry's financial strength and competitive environment. The industry should not make exaggerated promises or claim implausible achievements.

4. Member companies must create an effective internal implementation system to ensure effective code compliance.
5. Code compliance must be an integral part of a management performance evaluation and reward system.
6. The industry must create an independent governance structure that is not controlled by the executives of the member companies.
7. There must be an independent external monitoring and compliance verification system to engender public trust and credibility in the industry's claims of performance.
8. There should be maximum transparency and verifiable disclosure of industry performance to the public. Standards of performance disclosure should be the sole province of the code's governing board.

Our analysis conclusively demonstrate that HGPI Initiative fails to meet - even at the minimal level – any of these eight criteria. Therefore, the Initiative cannot and will not deliver on its promise of (a) improving GPO conduct, and (b) accurately reporting any changes in GPOs current conduct.

2. Do you believe the Industry Initiative has sufficient provisions to allow input from outside stakeholders, such as medical device manufacturers, physicians, hospitals and government officials? Do you believe outside stakeholders should have a role in evaluating GPO performance, and a role on the Industry Initiative's governance body?

The GPO Initiative makes only vague reference to getting outside input and only with regard to developing best business practices. The choice of outside stakeholders, the criteria for their selection, and the implementation of their advice, are left entirely to the discretion of the Initiative's Steering (Governance) Committee, which is comprised of the CEOs of member GPOs.

This is not the process that would attract serious and thoughtful input. The role of outsiders is of critical importance both at the governance level, and at the level of creating standards and measures of compliance, and independent external verification of such compliance.

In order to be effective and credible, the governance structure of the Initiative's governance body must not be controlled by the CEOs of the member GPOs. It has the appearance and potential for significant conflict of interest which must be avoided if the industry wants to engender public trust in its assertions of reform.

3. Please evaluate whether you believe each of the three legislative drafts circulated by the Subcommittee prior to the hearing are meritorious or not, and provide your reasons why. Please also provide any suggestions to improve each draft, should you have any.

See attached documents

4. Your written testimony states that you favor eliminating the GPO "safe harbor" which permits GPOs to accept fees from suppliers. Why do favor this approach? What is wrong with allowing vendors to fund GPOs?

The safe harbor provisions provide tremendous incentive to GPOs to maximize their profits and little or no incentives to relate the services rendered to income received. They have also had the effect of creating a highly concentrated oligapolistic structure where the top two companies control 60% of the market share.

The safe harbor has given rise to a system that is biased in favor of agency control and against stewardship. This can be evidenced from the following factors:

a) The fee structure of 3% is not related to costs or effectiveness, but is based on volume. This is best accomplished through selling the same product over a long period of time. All claims made by GPOs are based solely on the information provided by the GPOs. This information has not been independently monitored and verified. Therefore, when hospitals and other beneficiaries make claims of surpluses generated by their GPOs, they are based almost solely on the basis of information provided by the GPOs. There is no system that currently exists, which would allow these beneficiaries to determine for themselves as to whether the total savings claimed by the GPOs are indeed true; whether the operating costs of GPOs are reasonable, and whether the surplus distributed is reasonable and equitable.

b) GPOs also determine the adequacy of their operating costs (including top management compensation) and would be very reluctant to share this information.

c) GPOs' control of cost information, determination of surplus, and criteria for distributing this surplus to member hospitals, puts the beneficial owners (the hospitals) at the mercy of the GPOs (their agents). It also allows GPOs to make exaggerated and unverified claims about the reasonableness of their operating costs, the benefits accrued to hospitals through their negotiating skills and resulting in lower prices.

5. Would eliminating the safe harbor raise costs to individual hospitals, especially small ones, as suggested by Ms. Ubbing at the hearing?

This question is based on the false assumption that safe harbor is a free good and that its elimination would, therefore, deprive the hospitals – both large and small – from benefiting from this extra revenue. Nothing could be further from the truth.

The most important thing for the hospitals to understand and recognize is that the administrative fee is not some "free good" delivered by the suppliers out of the goodness of their heart. For them, it is just another cost of doing business. Someone must pay this cost and it is reflected in the price, at which these goods are sold by the suppliers. It should be apparent to everyone that GPOs' current suppliers are not running a charity and that any fee that they have to pay, no matter what it is called, eventually would have to be added to their costs and reflected in the prices they charge for their products. When this fee is eliminated, the money saved does not evaporate in thin air. It would either be reflected in lower prices charged by the suppliers, or someone else would have windfall profits. The inevitable result is that middlemen continue to earn enormous profits, and their managers excessive compensation, while hospitals struggle to make ends meet through excessive cost-cutting that often endangers the quality of service and patient care.

My extensive search of available information shows that GPOs have never made public any information that would objectively demonstrate their so-called savings to the hospitals, the reasonableness of the compensation paid to the GPO managers, and rationality of high level of operating expenses.

GPOs claims of the so-called savings are nothing more than unsubstantiated claims, which cannot be taken seriously when the cost of hospital supplies continues to rise and the revenues earned by GPOs also continue to increase.

SUBMISSIONS FOR THE RECORD

SUBCOMMITTEE ON ANTITRUST, COMPETITION POLICY AND CONSUMER RIGHTS, COMMITTEE ON THE JUDICIARY
UNITED STATES SENATE

TESTIMONY OF RICHARD J. BEDNAR
Coordinator, Healthcare Group Purchasing Industry Initiative
(Senior Counsel, Crowell & Moring LLP)
March 15, 2006

Good afternoon. I am Dick Bednar; the Coordinator of the Healthcare Group Purchasing Industry Initiative ("HGPII"), a position I have held since December 2005. I am pleased to report that this initiative is off and running on a sure path to success. We welcome this opportunity to tell you about this major GPO-industry development; a permanent, all voluntary, self-governing organization, committed to the highest level of ethical conduct in providing the best and safest products to patients, doctors and health care workers at competitive prices. In this testimony, I will be telling you a little about my qualifications as Coordinator, briefly describe the HGPII background, review quickly its guiding principles and public accountability process, mention achievements to date, explain our confidence that this GPO Initiative's self-governance process will work to assure ethical business conduct, and conclude by emphasizing the Initiative's transparency and public accountability. For brevity, I will refer to the Healthcare Group Purchasing Industry Initiative as the "GPO Initiative" or simply as "the Initiative".

COORDINATOR'S BACKGROUND

Before moving into the substance of this hearing, I want briefly to describe my qualifications. This is important because the Coordinator has a key role in assuring that the GPO Initiative is true to its commitments. I have had substantial experience evaluating, judging and helping frame organizational ethics and compliance programs. As the former Army debarring official, I often evaluated a government contractor's internal controls and ethical culture in deciding whether the contractor could be trusted as a government contracting partner. Second, as the current Coordinator of the Defense Industry Initiative on Business Ethics and Conduct ("DII"), I annually review each member company's certified and documented report of its ethics and conduct program to assure compliance with the DII principles. I also served recently on the Advisory Group to the U.S. Sentencing Commission on organizational sentencing guidelines, which resulted in congressionally approved changes effective November 2004. Chapter Eight of those guidelines lays out what many regard as the "gold standard" for all organizations to follow in developing programs to prevent and detect violations of law. Currently, I counsel clients on compliance matters as a significant part of my practice of law with Crowell & Moring LLP, where I have been since 1987.

HGPII PURPOSES, ORGANIZATION AND DEVELOPMENTS

The GPO Initiative has three main purposes. First, it is intended to nurture and to promote an ethical culture of compliance within every organization in the GPO industry. Second, the Initiative promotes self-governance as the means of confirming management's commitment to abide by ethical standards, and to discover and to correct instances where conduct falls below these standards. Third, the Initiative enforces a requirement that each organization in the GPO Initiative share best practices in dealing with ethics and business conduct issues. This sharing of practices is done both informally by communication among compliance officers as issues arise, and by participating in the annual "Best Practices Forum" at which the key compliance risk areas for the industry are openly discussed and internal control measures shared to reduce instances of noncompliance.

The GPO Initiative was founded in May of 2005 by the CEOs of nine of the nation's largest group purchasing organizations. The Initiative's founding members are Amerinet, Broadlane, Child Health Corporation of America, Consorta, GNYHA Ventures, Inc., Healthtrust Purchasing Group, MedAssets Supply Chain Systems, Novation and Premier. These organizations represent an estimated 80 percent or more of the volume of purchases through GPOs.

The Steering Committee is the governing body of the GPO Initiative and functions like a board of directors. The Steering Committee is comprised of the CEOs of the nine founding GPO members. There also is a Working Group, which works with the Coordinator in carrying out the day-to-day GPO Initiative programs and activities.

The GPO Initiative is modeled after the respected Defense Industry Initiative on Business Ethics and Conduct (DII), with which I am confidently familiar. The DII is widely held to be a success story. The DII was established in June 1986 by the CEOs of a small group of large defense companies. The DII has grown to over 65 companies, and continues to experience strong public and government confidence in its sincere commitment to the highest ethical and conduct standards.

The Initiative I am reporting on today, the GPO Initiative, is the result of many months of careful study and planning during the period of March 2002 to May 2005. The GPO Initiative is by no measure a hastily prepared "Quick Fix." To the contrary, countless hours of study, reviews, reflection and consulting with outside ethics experts, like Dr. Kirk O. Hanson of the Markula Center for Applied Ethics, Santa Clara University, have gone into establishment of this permanent institution. The GPO Initiative was encouraged by the members and staff of this Subcommittee in discussions and appearances during 2002 through 2004. For example, at the September 14, 2004 hearing, Chairman DeWine suggested that the GPO industry could set up a "voluntary plus" approach, pursuant to which voluntary adherence to ethics codes would be enforced as a continuing effort. In the spirit of that encouragement, the CEOs of the nine founding GPOs agreed on deliberate purposes, and otherwise shaped the organization of the GPO Initiative, centered on a strong commitment to ethical business practices and demonstrated by transparency.

In February of 2005, as GPO Initiative neared its formal launch, representatives met with Chairman De Wine and Senator Kohl to report on progress toward founding of the GPO Initiative. Throughout the development, the GPO Initiative has kept the staff of the Subcommittee informed of its progress. The unmistakable objective of the GPO Initiative is that it is a permanent institution, dedicated to the continuous improvement of policies and practices in the industry, and within a culture of compliance.

The GPO Initiative requires each signatory company to pledge to follow six core ethical principles, to report annually on adherence to these principles using a Public Accountability Questionnaire, and to participate with other GPO representatives and other interested parties in an annual Best Practices Forum on business conduct practices.

The six principles are:

(1) Each Signatory shall have and adhere to a written code of business conduct. The code establishes high ethical values and sound business practices for the Signatory's group purchasing organization.

(2) Each Signatory shall train all within the organization as to their personal responsibilities under the code.

(3) Each Signatory commits itself to work toward the twin goals of high quality healthcare and cost effectiveness.

(4) Each Signatory commits itself to work toward an open and competitive purchasing process free of conflicts of interest and any undue influences.

(5) Each Signatory shall have the responsibility to each other to share their best practices in implementing the Principles; each Signatory shall participate in an annual Best Practices Forum.

(6) Each Signatory, through its participation in this Initiative, shall be accountable to the public.

BEST PRACTICES FORUM

On January 11, 2006, the GPO Initiative held its second Steering Committee meeting. All nine of the founding CEOs personally attended that meeting, where the course was set for the rest of this year.

Then, on January 12 and 13, 2006, the Initiative held its initial Best Practices Forum; the agenda has been provided for the record. About 100 registrants participated in the Forum, including all nine of the founding CEOs, and many senior GPO executives. The discussion was open, frank and substantive. The discussion ranged from competitive award strategies, to handling vendor grievances, to encouraging breakthrough technology, to avoiding conflicts of interest, and to further promoting small business and diversity initiatives.

As a direct result of the Forum, the participants have established two working committees, one to address compliance; the second to address diversity and small business matters.

I am very pleased to repeat that this GPO Initiative is off and running on a path destined for success.

PUBLIC ACCOUNTABILITY

The Annual Accountability process requires each organization to respond publicly to a 19 item questionnaire and provide electronic links to backup internal policies and procedures, which also are available to the public. This accountability process addresses such questions as whether the organization has and adheres to a code of conduct; whether it follows appropriate conflict of interest policies; and whether its policies regarding administrative fees and bundling are free from provisions that create inappropriate incentives. These are merely examples of the probing questions which must be answered and documented. We have submitted copies of the Initiative Charter and Annual Public Accountability Questionnaire for the record, and these are available publicly on the GPO Initiatives' website.

These documented responses annually are provided to me as the Coordinator, who has the responsibility for making an independent, detailed review. When I am satisfied that the responses demonstrate the commitment the GPO Initiative expects of all its members, I will approve each answer as responsive, complete, and fairly given. Once approved, the responses to the questionnaires are individually posted on the Initiative website: www.healthcaregpoii.com.

In responding to the Annual Public Accountability Questionnaire, each organization must reveal substantial detail about its business policies and practices. The degree of transparency required by the Annual Public Accountability Questionnaire is extensive and, to my knowledge, unprecedented in the voluntary practices of any other industry. For example, each company describes its practices in such areas as (i) disclosure of requirements for vendors to be acceptable identified as potential bidders; (ii) a fair and unbiased system for evaluating products and services considered for procurement; (iii) standards for appropriate use of sole, single and multi-source procurement; (iv) an approach to administrative fees which insures that the interests of the GPO do not supplant those of the member organizations; and (v) guidance for appropriate bundling of products and the length of contracts. Each company must also provide adequate supporting documentation to permit the Coordinator to determine that each answer to the questionnaire is responsive, complete, and fairly given. This public disclosure of ethical and business conduct practices, which the GPOs believe assure adherence to the Initiative's six core principles, will open the responses of these practices for all to see and judge.

SELF GOVERNANCE WILL WORK

Having described the purposes, the organization, and the accountability process, I now move on to describe why we believe this self-governance process will work.

There are several ways in which the GPO Initiative shapes ethical practices. First, it is expected that participation in the Initiative itself will become a key criteria for hospitals and other providers when selecting membership in a GPO. In fact, hospitals already have begun to require that a GPO be a participant in the Initiative as a condition for that hospital's participation in a GPO. The American Hospital Association, Association of American Medical

Colleges, Catholic Health Association of the United States, Federation of American Hospitals, National Association of Children's Hospitals, National Association of Public Hospitals and Health Systems and the National Rural Health Association, have endorsed this process. Being acutely concerned about the integrity of their supply chain, we expect that hospital boards of directors will look for positive assurance that their GPO is committed to and is monitoring its own ethical behavior. Participation in the GPO Initiative will provide that assurance.

Second, participating GPO organizations are required to enlarge their ethical and business conduct practices as necessary in order to respond affirmatively to each of the questions in the Annual Public Accountability Questionnaire. This has led all participating GPOs to examine their own practices to assure that they adhere to the GPO Initiative principles.

Third, the executives and boards of the hospital systems will be able to scrutinize the specific practices of the GPO to which they belong and compare those practices with other GPOs outside of the GPO Initiative. This competitive pressure will give providers leverage to encourage, and even, to demand, changes to GPO business practices.

Fourth, the disclosure of each organization's practices to the public will bring a level of visibility not present in any other industry. This will allow scrutiny by the press, by those who may be skeptical, and by this Subcommittee of the business policies and practices of the GPOs. The transparency will further assure GPO business practices are in harmony with the expectations of the Congress and the public.

Fifth, key practices, particularly those where there may be significant differences, are to be discussed at each annual Best Practices Forum openly in front of their peers and invited guests. Practices considered "best" by the Working Group and the Coordinator will be featured and information will be available regarding how to implement featured best practices. In this regard, persons outside of the Initiative will be invited to participate in all future Best Practices Forums.

Sixth, we expect that over time the policies and practices required to justify continued participation in the GPO Initiative will evolve and strengthen. The standard expected in response to each Public Accountability Questionnaire will rise, creating a virtuous cycle which raises the practices of all companies in the industry.

While the central focus of the Initiative is to encourage good ethical practices, there is a procedure for suspending a GPO's participation or membership in the Initiative of any GPO which fails to fulfill its obligations under the Initiative. I believe this step will be a rare one, as the stigma and competitive impact of being suspended from the GPO Initiative would be substantial. Instead, I expect that encouragement by peer CEOs and the Coordinator will readily resolve any perceived shortcomings in the commitment to the Initiatives principles. Should a serious ethical failure equate to criminal or civil misconduct, there are ample means already in existence to address such failures.

THE GPO INITIATIVE IS IN HARMONY WITH THE PUBLIC'S DEMAND FOR SELF-GOVERNANCE

The self-governance undergirding of this Initiative is in harmony with the wave of expectations for self-governance currently nudging all organizations. I refer to the explicit and implicit guidance in the Sarbanes-Oxley Act, the Rules of the New York Stock Exchange, Chapter 8 of the U.S. Sentencing Commission Guidelines for Organizations, the January 2003 memorandum from the Deputy Attorney General of the United States stating compliance expectations, to the Standards of Conduct Regulations of the Department of Defense, HHS, and other federal agencies. These authorities all recognize that the willingness to follow ethical practices arises out of an organizational culture of compliance, rather than from unwelcomed restraints imposed by external rules. Behavior follows expectations, and the GPO Initiative's expectations are high.

Additionally self-governance keeps GPOs focused on best practices, not minimal compliance with regulations. Unfortunately, it is an unavoidable outcome of regulation that the focus tends to shift to satisfying the letter of the law rather than its spirit.

Self-governance also can better address the existing differences between the business models of the various GPOs. Some GPOs are stand-alone enterprises and some are subsidiaries of larger entities; some GPOs package broad consulting services with purchasing while others do purchasing only. This means that their customers, i.e. health care providers, have a wide variety of choices about how they can purchase their supplies efficiently. The extensive information about GPOs that will be available publicly through the Initiative will permit healthcare providers to easily compare GPOs and select the model or models that best suit their needs.

We believe that achieving exemplary ethics and business practices across an industry is something that will occur only if the leadership of the industry makes a significant commitment to achieve the articulated standards. With this Initiative, each CEO is pledging that his or her organization will achieve the ethical and business conduct standards that are addressed in the core principles and the questionnaire, and will do so with extraordinary transparency. Each participating GPO will do this because they have chosen to do it voluntarily.

This voluntary, self-governance initiative is the best way to achieve lasting change.

THE FUTURE

The Congress can expect continued transparency from the GPO Initiative, and significant open debate about particular practices in the GPO industry. This will demonstrate that the Initiative is working as planned. The transparent scrutiny and debate over practices will be what assures a culture of compliance within the industry.

While the nine initial original members of the GPO Initiative represent the overwhelming majority of volume handled by GPOs, it is important to invite all other GPOs to join. We have already opened the door to other GPOs to join in this initiative – these invitations have resulted in new members, including one based in Canada, and have already generated a productive dialogue about the Initiative, its accomplishments, and its plans. A broader invitation is planned for the coming months, so that new Initiative members can participate in the next Best Practices Forum, to be presented in January of 2007.

It is also important that the transparency and scrutiny of practices made possible by the Initiative be extended to other parts of the healthcare industry supply chain. I understand that there is substantial concern about the practices in links in the supply chain other than GPOs. Our vision is that a similar ethics initiative featuring extensive transparency and regular accountability will eventually be embraced and practiced by other components of the healthcare industry.

We believe that this permanent, voluntary effort will serve the goals so strongly advocated by members of this Subcommittee, and fully embraced by the GPOs which formed the Initiative. Through communication among GPO Initiative members, the industry and this

Subcommittee, and by continued transparency, we are confident that the Initiative will result in a GPO industry that warrants the trust and confidence of the public and of the hospitals and the communities they serve.

Thank you.

RICHARD BLUMENTHAL
ATTORNEY GENERAL

55 Elm Street
P.O. Box 120
Hartford, CT 06141-0120

Office of The Attorney General

State of Connecticut

TESTIMONY OF
ATTORNEY GENERAL RICHARD BLUMENTHAL
BEFORE THE ANTITRUST, COMPETITION POLICY AND CONSUMER RIGHTS SUBCOMMITTEE OF THE SENATE JUDICIARY COMMITTEE
MARCH 15, 2006

I appreciate the opportunity to submit testimony on the subject of federal regulation of hospital group purchasing organizations (GPOs)

My investigation of GPO abuses and irregularities was spurred by credible and now well-documented reports of GPO misuse of their purchasing power and the member hospitals' failures to accurately account for GPO revenues Evidence from my investigation, and yours, supports aggressive Congressional action addressing such anti-consumer abuses.

Equally worthy of attention is possible action concerning an organization that I am investigating as part of my GPO investigation The organization -- the Healthcare Research and Development Institute (HRDI) -- is a secretive for-profit company composed of a network of healthcare corporate executives as well as manufacturers and suppliers of medical and health care related goods and services that may well raise anti-competitive concerns. At the very least, it suggests insider dealings -- an insidious, incestuous, insider system -- symptomatic of the GPO industry.

Like the GPOs, its business model appears to rely on apparently opaque and ethically questionable business arrangements, as well as potentially anti-competitive business practices that these hearings and the proposed legislation seek to address and remedy.

HRDI is neither a trade organization nor a GPO It is a for-profit limited liability company owned by leading chief executive officers of major hospitals and healthcare systems across the country. HRDI also comprises 45 or so "corporate members" who apply for membership in HRDI and, if accepted, pay significant annual dues and possibly additional fees These corporate members are a "Who's Who" in the healthcare manufacturing, medical device and health services fields, including Becton Dickinson, Sodexho Healthcare, Heidrick & Struggles and MedAssets, a large GPO

Organized over fifty years ago, HRDI claims a laudable purpose -- to provide a forum for these leading healthcare executives to "come together" with their corporate partners to "share . . . ideas and strategies, . . seek ways to improve their hospitals and systems" and "to educate healthcare companies who serve the industry" in order to ensure their products and services "better meet patient and provider needs." HRDI's structure, fee schedules, compensation practices and its limited and exclusive corporate membership appear to belie its stated purpose.

Simply put, HRDI provides its corporate members with the opportunity to purchase special access to hospital and healthcare system CEOs. These CEOs are in a position to directly or indirectly exert considerable influence on purchasing decisions relating to the products that the corporate members sell to the hospitals and health systems these CEOs represent.

The annual dues these corporate members pay to HRDI are used to compensate the CEOs for their "services" to the corporate membership.

HRDI subscribes to a "Rule of Two". Its corporate membership is limited to two members in any particular category of product or service. For example, only two pharmaceutical wholesalers or two manufacturers of safety needles would be admitted. This, too, may raise anti-competitive concerns.

All of HRDI's activities -- meetings and educational events that it sponsors -- are cloaked in secrecy. Members of this subcommittee who visit HRDI's website at www.HRDI.com will find a website that is inaccessible to everyone but its corporate and individual members. You will be unable to identify HRDI's individual members, corporate members, upcoming meetings, or anything else, for that matter. It leads me to question whether the boards of directors for the hospitals and healthcare systems where these CEOs work -- as well as state regulators -- are aware of HRDI's activities, and precisely how much its individual members earn for their "services" to the corporate members.

To date, HRDI and its members have cooperated in my investigation. Nevertheless, my GPO investigation has broadened to determine whether HRDI serves to perpetuate the "pay-to-play" scheme that has infected so much of the healthcare industry, through GPOs, pharmaceutical benefit managers and the pharmaceutical marketers.

Many GPOs are owned by consortiums of hospitals and major medical supply purchasers. They channel their purchasing power to obtain volume discounts and rebates from suppliers. They also receive administrative fees from the suppliers in return for the ability to sell their products to the GPO members through GPO-negotiated contracts.

My GPO investigation has uncovered suspect interrelationships and questionable business practices involving hospital, GPO and major medical supplier executives whose practices often benefit themselves, rather than patients, insurers and government programs that pay hospital bills.

Specifically, my office in cooperation with the state Medicaid agency has determined that some Connecticut Medicaid providers -- nursing homes, that purchase health care supplies through contracts negotiated by their GPO -- have not properly accounted for rebates received in connection with these purchases. The improper allocation of rebates, as well as discounts, fees and other incentives through these financials arrangements, have possibly increased costs to the Medicaid program. My office will continue to investigate these issues.

The preliminary findings of my investigation mirror the conclusions of two recent reports from the Office of the Inspector General of the Department of Health and Human Services (OIG). These reports -- auditing 6 GPOs practices over a 3-5 year period -- found that many member hospitals failed to properly account for more than $60 million in rebates and other payments from the GPOs that medical suppliers paid.

The OIG reports raise a third major concern -- whether the GPOs' retention of almost $500 million dollars for 'investment and reserve' purposes is a valid use of their member hospitals resources. Many of them are non-profit organizations.

As I stated in my previous testimony before the committee, I have a longstanding concern that GPOs create a myriad of conflicts of interest and anti-competitive behavior that must be regulated, if not prohibited. Certainly, this conclusion is supported by a recent jury antitrust award to Masimo Corporation, a producer of pulse oximetry devices, of $420 million in damages against Tyco Healthcare Group and its affiliate, Mallinckrodt. The jury found that Tyco and Mallinckrodt used sole-source/high compliance contracts and bundled rebates to bar competitors, such as Masimo, from obtaining business from major hospital groups.

In sum, these concerns are significant and serious, requiring immediate Congressional action. Voluntary efforts offered by the GPO companies -- initiated shortly after withering criticism of industry practices -- are simply too little, too late.

I urge the committee to adopt legislation similar to Senator Herb Kohl and Senator Mike DeWine's Medical Device Competition Act of 2004. This legislation: (1) caps GPO administrative fees at 3% of the purchase price of the good or service; and (2) requires the Secretary of Health and Human Services, in consultation with the United States Attorney General and the Federal Trade Commission, to issue regulations on specifying purchasing practices that violate antitrust laws or ethical standards and prohibiting certain forms of payments and tightening the definition of what is acceptable compensation.

In addition, I reiterate my recommendations from last year. The committee should consider legislation to:

- Eliminate conflicts of interest in this industry by prohibiting GPOs and health care-related supply, medical device and equipment companies from having any ownership interest in each other. In addition, no member of a board of directors, officer, individual with contracting authority or owner of more than 5% of a GPO should have any ownership interest in health care-related supply and medical device and equipment companies.

- Strictly and vigorously prohibit any GPO from accepting any fees from vendors in excess of 3 percent of the purchase price of goods or services sold to members by these vendors. Excessive fees, and other reimbursements such as stock options may rise to the level of an improper inducement to influence a GPO's selection of vendors for its supply contracts, which poses potential conflicts of interest for the GPO, unfairly excludes smaller vendors from the contracting process and possibly taints the vendor selection process, which ultimately may lead to higher prices or substandard products

- Require GPOs to report to the Department of Health and Human Services all fees or other remuneration from vendors. This information should arguably be kept confidential only if it clearly constitutes a trade secret. Such reporting will assist the Department in monitoring compliance with the fee limits

- Require that a GPO disclose to its hospital members any and all information concerning the quality, safety and efficacy of the products purchased from a health care-related supply, medical device or equipment company.

- Prohibit any GPO contract provision that prohibits or penalizes a member from testing or gaining information about a clinical preference item offered by a vendor that does not currently have a contract with the GPO.

- Prohibit sole source contracts by GPOs for clinical preference items unless there is no other means of obtaining such products. Health care providers should be able to access the most effective medical devices and products where there are valid, documented clinical preferences for more than one type of such medical device or product.

- Prohibit GPOs from tying or bundling products in a manner that unreasonably restricts competition or clinical preferences for medical equipment or devices.

- Limit GPO contracts with health care-related supply, medical device and equipment companies to no more than 3 years in order to encourage competition in the medical supply and product industries. Long-term contracts, especially by larger GPOs, can restrict competition by limiting the market for competing products.

- Require the Federal Trade Commission to promulgate regulations within two years of the effective date of the legislation to ensure robust competition in the GPO, hospital purchasing and medical supply industries

- Require each GPO to designate a compliance officer to monitor the GPO's compliance with federal regulations and laws governing GPO practices.

In addition to legislative changes, the subcommittee should urge more aggressive federal action to investigate and prosecute antitrust violations by GPOs, particularly in light of *LePage's v. 3M Corp.*, which supports and encourages such antitrust enforcement against health care product bundling and other anticompetitive abuses. The effectiveness of any law depends on tough, sustained enforcement.

I will continue to move aggressively in my investigation and look forward to working with the committee in its legislative efforts.

Senator Brownback

Hospital Group Purchasing Organizations

I support the Healthcare Group Purchasing Industry Initiative. This initiative assures us that GPOs are holding themselves to the highest of standards. Accordingly, I recognize that government intervention has the potential to suppress innovation in our health care system.

A recent study determined that the cost savings to hospitals utilizing GPOs is between 10-15 percent. That translates into a savings of between $187 and $332 million for health care in the state of Kansas. As Congress examines ways to lower the costs of health care, I think we can all agree that a cost savings of $332 million is significant to our health care system.

The Child Health Corporation of America, headquartered in Shawnee Mission, Kansas, is a Group Purchasing Organization that represents children's hospitals across the country. CHCA's owner-hospitals include over 20,000 physicians and 100,000 employees in 22 states.

CHCA spends time in the market, advocating for the needs of children's hospitals – something that an individual children's hospital would not have the time or resources to do. For instance, CHCA sponsored a forum of pharmacists to discuss common issues. One great idea that came out of this forum was to educate pharmacists on the need to include more child dosage information on certain medications. These kinds of discussions are leading to new and better ways to improve the quality of our nation's health care system.

We need to allow the Group Purchasing Industry Initiative to work. With full disclosure, the market will play a strong role in deciding if there are any bad actors in the industry.

To the Members of the Senate Subcommittee on Antitrust, Competition Policy and Consumer Rights,

No one has to tell you about the aging baby boomer population and the enormous financial challenges they present to the Medicare program. Every real dollar saved is critical to the program's survival. As you prepare for the upcoming GPO hearing I would ask you to focus on the heart of the matter. This is really about much more than codes of conduct or new GPO lobbying organizations or new coats of paint. The real issue is this. Do GPOs really save money? If it can be proven beyond a shadow of a doubt that they do, then they should be allowed to continue their work under the current system. If their claimed cost savings cannot be proven, then they do not deserve special protections from the governmen and they should not be allowed to legally collect fees from suppliers that in any other industry would be called bribes. But regardless of what the fees are called or that they are made legal through legislation, without strong oversight human nature will insure that the outcome of those fees will be the same as the outcome achieved through illegal bribes and kickbacks. Without real measurable proof of cost savings the Safe Harbor becomes nothing more than a taxpayer funded entitlement program for GPOs.

Procurement is all about numbers. Cost either go up, go down or stay the same. And it can all be quantified with good accounting. Procurement managers at companies across the world know that their jobs depend on their ability to produce real cost savings and prove their results using real numbers. Surely the bar for GPOs should not be lower. So why is it so hard for GPOs to prove that they save money?

Here is what the evidence says:

1. GPOs claim huge cost savings but have never provided real proof of even a single dollar of real savings.
2. Hospitals, in general, cannot quantify the savings from their GPO without the GPO telling them what they saved. But the GPOs don't provide proof, just marketing spin and an annual rebate check that looks and spends like savings but can't possibly be savings because it can only be funded by the inflated prices the hospitals themselves pay. But there is another problem with what is known as excess fees disbursement. This is a benefit reserved for shareholders only so they receive fee money that was earned not by their purchasing volume alone but also the purchasing volume of the non shareholder members who do not share in this excess fee distribution. But becoming a shareholder often requires the payment of an enormous fee that the hospital may not be able to recoop if it leaves the GPO.
3. The GAO's own study indicated that GPOs don't save money.
4. Supply costs continue to rise year after year with no end in sight.
5. It has been documented by the GAO that GPOs collect enormous amounts of money from large suppliers, a cost that must be built into the price of the products hospitals buy and passed on to state and federal governments and taxpayers.

To your credit you have been thoughtful and deliberate in your approach to this issue. You have given the GPOs ample opportunity to prove their value and address their business practices. Self imposed codes of conduct may make the outside of the house look better but have no effect on what takes place inside the home. Likewise a new paint job on a car will not fix the cracked cylinder head under the hood.

No doubt you are receiving letters from hospital CEOs predicting their rapid demise if the Safe Harbor goes away. But hospitals have always been free to engage the services of outside groups to assist them in their cost cutting efforts and removing the Safe Harbor will not jeopardize that ability. As you read each of those hospital letters I would urge you to consider the following. If GPOs provided real savings to their members hospitals would not be able sign up fast enough. And they would find a way to pay for it and would be able to afford to do so because of the savings enjoyed and there would be no need for a Safe Harbor. If you audited any hospital regarding how they spend their money I am sure you would find many expenditures on things far less important than the CEOs say their GPOs are to their ability to continue their mission of providing quality and affordable health care.

Barring eleventh hour proof of real savings, it is time to remove the Safe Harbor and restore competition to the health care supply chain. A return to a competition rich free market approach will ultimately lower supply costs and make the government's job of adequately funding Medicare easier. Otherwise, supply costs will continue to rise without abatement and more and more citizens will find it harder to get the care they need at an affordable price. And how will the government meet its obligations to its Medicare recipients if this is allowed to continue?

Sincerely,

Lynn James Everard
Healthcare Strategist

March 29, 2006

The Honorable Mike DeWine, Chairman
Senate Subcommittee on Antitrust, Competition
Policy and Consumer Rights
140 Russell Senate Office Building
Washington, DC 20510

The Honorable Herb Kohl, Ranking Member
Senate Subcommittee on Antitrust, Competition
Policy and Consumer Rights
330 Hart Senate Office Building
Washington, DC 20510

Dear Senators DeWine and Kohl:

We are responding to your letter of March 15, 2006 requesting comment on three draft bills relating to hospital group purchasing organizations ("GPOs"): (1) the "Medical Device Competition Act" ("S.2880"); (2) the "Hospital Group Purchasing Organization Reform Act"; and (3) the "Ensuring Competition in Hospital Purchasing Act."

GPOs provide procurement vehicles and information empowering hospitals to purchase medical equipment and supplies at substantially reduced group rates. In addition to these direct savings, GPOs relieve hospitals of the costs of staffing for acquisition planning, market research, and purchasing. At the same time, hospitals remain free to purchase directly from vendor sources and to change GPOs, thus promoting competition. Vendors who choose to sell through GPOs capitalize on volume and on being relieved of the costs of marketing and selling. The Health Group Purchasing Industry Initiative (HGPII) now underlies this process by assuring the public interest in transparency and accountability for ethical business practices.

As you will both recall, Ms. Mina Ubbing, CEO of the Fairfield Medical Center in Lancaster, Ohio, testified that legislation is not in the best interest of the hospitals. That position is shared by the Ohio and Wisconsin Hospital Associations. Hospitals today have access to over 30 GPOs each with different business models, product offerings and expertise. There is significant competition among the GPOs for each hospital's business, assuring hospitals the opportunity to change if they are not satisfied with the GPO's performance. More importantly, every decision on what the hospital will buy is made by that hospital. Each hospital is able to evaluate any and all technologies, innovations, improvements or modifications, based on its own priorities and that of its physicians. GPOs do not make clinical purchasing decisions for their hospitals.

The above mentioned regulations would deny hospitals a highly competitive GPO industry which is a key to providing high value to the hospitals. In general, these bills would impose a complex, burdensome, expensive and unprecedented web of regulations, certifications and attendant criminal liability on GPOs and other purchasing agents. As a result, these regulations would—among other things—substantially increase (1) the direct supply chain management costs to hospitals and other health care organizations, and (2) the indirect health care costs to patients and payers, including the federal government. For example, a study of the industry estimates that these bills would increase total direct U.S. health care spending by between $23.9 billion and $34.6 billion over ten years. The cost to Medicare and Medicaid over the same ten year period is estimated at between $8.2 billion and $9.7 billion. These increased expenses and burdensome regulations would fall most heavily on small and rural hospitals.

Hospitals will directly suffer from this straightjacket approach to group purchasing that would result from the bureaucracy created by these bills. A one-size-fits-all GPO framework would stifle the current competitive environment that encourages innovative solutions and creative efforts to further increase savings and improve clinical outcomes.

It is important to note that these legislative options are being considered at a time when hospitals are increasingly being challenged to control costs while concurrently improving patient care. Hospitals have never been under such pressure to provide unlimited care on a limited budget. They face uninsured patients, an aging population, reimbursement cuts, staff shortages and a list of problems that all require monetary resources. GPOs exist to help hospitals improve patient care and control health care costs; GPOs are succeeding in this mission and are doing so with greater transparency than ever before. These legislative proposals would severely limit, if not eliminate altogether, the ability of GPOs to provide to our hospital clients, including small and rural hospitals, the purchasing power that enables them to buy expensive equipment and critical supplies at group discount rates.

In addition, the proposed legislation is unnecessary. A July 2004 report on the U.S. healthcare industry by the Department of Justice Antitrust Division and the Federal Trade Commission concluded that no new regulation of GPOs is needed and that those agencies have sufficient authority to safeguard competition in the future. In fact, no federal agency has called for or supported legislation to further regulate GPOs following this thorough examination of the hospital group purchasing organization industry.

Industry self-governance efforts have already made substantial progress toward increasing transparency and sharing best ethical business practices, and have completed a cycle of public disclosure. In consultation with the Subcommittee, both the GPO industry, through the Healthcare Group Purchasing Industry Initiative ("HGPII"), and individual GPOs, have established—and are implementing—detailed codes of conduct that address each of the principal concerns raised both by the Subcommittee and other interested parties. This self-governance effort has made substantial progress. Among other things, HGPII—which was founded by the nine undersigned GPOs—has (1) adopted a core set of principles of business conduct and ethics; (2) adopted a detailed (and publicly available), 19-part "Annual Public Accountability Questionnaire" that must be completed by each HGPII member, reviewed by the company CEOs and validated by the HGPII Coordinator; (3) posted each member's 2005 response to the Questionnaire on HGPII's web site; and (4) in January 2006, held its first annual "Best Practices Forum," which was attended by approximately 100 industry leaders. We firmly believe that the voluntary approach represented by HGPII is the most efficient and effective method to promote and monitor best ethical and business practices, and that the Subcommittee should allow the Initiative an opportunity to accomplish its mission of self-governance.

Our more specific comments on each of the bills are set forth on the following pages.

Medical Device Competition Act (S.2880)

This bill would amend the federal, criminal health care program anti-kickback law ("Anti-Kickback Law") and, more specifically, the Law's exception for fees paid by vendors to group purchasing organizations ("GPO Safe Harbor"). We oppose this bill for many reasons, including the following:

- First, the bill would limit vendor fees to an amount equal to the "reasonable costs associated with the procurement of products and the administration of valid contracts." This language would impede GPOs from funding activities that provide economies of scale or efficiencies for the supply chain, which includes research or programs in areas such as data standards, patient safety, electronic commerce and education and advocacy for best practices. Finally, the language would eliminate any distributions to the hospitals. As you know, GPOs' direct financial support to hospitals, including rural hospitals, is very significant and important to them.
- Second, the bill broadly prohibits payments from vendors that "include marketing costs, any extraneous fees, or any other payment intended to unduly or improperly influence the award of a contract based on factors other than the cost, quality, safety, or efficacy of the product." Like the previous provision, the terms used here—such as "extraneous," "unduly" and "improperly"—are undefined, vague and ambiguous and would, as such, create expansive and unwarranted criminal exposure for thousands of individuals and organizations. In addition, this provision is unworkable in practice. For example, vendor fee provisions are set forth in the GPO-vendor agreement, and it is impossible to know at the time such an agreement is being negotiated whether, during the term of the agreement, the fee set forth therein ultimately will or will not be equal to the "reasonable" costs to the GPO that are "associated" with the procurement of products under (and/or the administration of) the agreement.
- Third, the bill would require the U.S. Department of Health & Human Services ("HHS") to promulgate regulations that specify "contracting," "business" and "ethical" practices that are "contrary to antitrust laws and competitive principles, to ethical standards, or to the goal of ensuring that products necessary for proper patient care or worker safety are readily available to physicians, health care workers, and

patients." This provision would give unprecedented, inappropriate and unrequested new regulatory powers to the Department of Health and Human Services for the first time in its history. The bill also would require GPOs to comply with these regulations in order to be protected by the GPO Safe Harbor and, thereby, to avoid criminal prosecution. Manifestly, this provision both (1) is impossibly and unworkably broad from a regulatory development standpoint, and (2) is overly inclusive in terms of creating criminal liability.

- Fourth, the bill would require that HHS annually certify that every GPO and other "purchasing agent" are in compliance with each of the new regulations discussed above. The bill defines "purchasing agent," in turn, as including "any individual, organization, or other entity that negotiates and implements contracts to purchase hospital supplies or medical equipment, devices, products, goods or services of any kind for any group of individuals or entities who are furnishing services reimbursable under a Federal health care program, including organizations commonly known as 'group purchasing organizations.'" Even without this expansive definition of "purchasing agent"—which probably includes tens of thousands of individuals, distributors, Integrated Delivery Networks (IDNs) and other entities—this provision would impose an extreme, unnecessary and unprecedented burden on both HHS and GPOs.
- Fifth, a recent analysis of the provisions of S.2880 by Muse & Associates concludes that the bill would increase healthcare costs in the United States by $29.3 billion to $34.6 billion over a ten-year period. Within that overall cost increase, Medicare and Medicaid costs would increase between $8.2 billion and $9.7 billion over the same ten year period.
- Sixth, this proposal and the other proposals under consideration by the Subcommittee are not necessary because the antitrust enforcement agencies (FTC and DOJ) and other federal and state regulatory agencies already have and exercise the authority to protect competition, patient care, and worker safety. In July 2004, the FTC and DOJ jointly issued a publication based on 27 days of FTC /DOJ Joint Hearings on Health Care and Competition Law and Policy, held from February through October 2003; an FTC sponsored workshop in September 2002; and independent research. The hearings gathered testimony and written comments from more than 300 participants, including representatives of various provider groups, insurers, employers, lawyers, patient advocates, and leading scholars on subjects ranging from antitrust and economics to health care, quality and informed consent. The FTC panel voted unanimously to approve the findings of the report.

  In the report, these federal agencies themselves concluded that the Safety Zone provision of Statement 7 does not protect anticompetitive contracting practices of group purchasing organizations and that it does not preclude agency action challenging anticompetitive practices. Both agencies have actively reviewed the industry, and private litigation is taking place to enforce the antitrust laws. The agencies themselves have stated that authority already exists to challenge improper GPO behavior. Lastly, concerns about "proper patient care and worker safety" are already addressed by separate legal regimes (for example, OIG-HHS, OSHA, JCAHO accreditation, malpractice law) and hospitals, and GPOs face intense market pressures to ensure patient care and worker safety (for example, competition for doctors and patients, malpractice exposure and insurance costs, and labor pressures.).

Hospital Group Purchasing Organization Reform Act

This bill also would amend the Anti-Kickback Law's GPO Safe Harbor. We also oppose this bill for many reasons, including the following:

- First, like S.2880, this bill effectively (1) would restrict vendor fees to those that were "reasonably associated with the procurement of products or the administration of valid contracts" and (2) would ban payments "intended to unduly or improperly influence the award of a contract based on factors other than the cost, quality, safety, or efficacy of the product." For the reasons set forth above, these provisions are vague, ambiguous and unworkable in practice.
- Second, the bill would require GPOs to have a code of conduct with provisions that, among other things, would "prevent business practices which are contrary to the goal of ensuring that the best and safest products are available to physicians, health care workers, and patients at a competitive price." This is an unworkable and vague standard. As you are aware, every competing vendor believes its products to be the best and safest products and always provides to potential purchasers product materials that the vendor believes to support its claim. Further, each hospital has its own view and, for this reason, often will not purchase the GPO contracted product. Finally, there is a wide variety of views among clinicians and health care workers with respect to many products. We do not believe this to be an appropriate framework for a criminal statute or even a regulatory scheme. (A GPO without such a code of conduct—or not in "substantial" compliance with such code of conduct—would not be eligible for protection under the GPO Safe Harbor and, as such, would be subject to criminal prosecution.) Like its counterpart in S.2880, this provision is overly broad and would impose an unprecedented burden on GPOs. Indeed, while there are a number of industries—most notably the pharmaceutical industry—that have a self-imposed self-governance compliance mechanism (similar to, but less expansive than, HGPII's Charter and its guiding Principles), we are not aware of any providers, suppliers or practitioners who are subject, by statute or regulation, to a government-imposed code of conduct as potentially sweeping and burdensome as that being proposed in this bill.
- Third, the bill calls for the creation of a new "Hospital Group Purchasing Organizations Ethics and Business Practices Compliance Office" ("Office") within HHS. The Office would be required, among other things, to (1) annually certify that each GPO's code of conduct meets statutory and regulatory requirements and that the organization is in substantial compliance with its code of conduct, and (2) solicit the views of "all interested parties, including suppliers or manufacturers of medical products, medical equipment, or medical devices," when making this certification. For the reasons discussed above, this provision would impose an extreme, unnecessary and unprecedented burden on HHS and GPOs. It also would be both

unfair and unprecedented to permit vendors to play an active role in the government's regulation and certification of GPOs. GPOs work for their hospital and the patients they serve.

<u>Ensuring Competition in Hospital Purchasing Act</u>

This bill would eliminate the AntiKickback Law's GPO Safe Harbor. The direct result of eliminating the GPO Safe Harbor, in turn, would be a substantial increase in the supply chain costs of hospitals, particularly hospitals in rural areas and underserved communities. The reasons for this are several-fold:

- First, the complex process of (1) developing and drafting requests for proposal; (2) soliciting responsive bids from prospective vendors; (3) analyzing these bids to determine which offer the best combination of clinical value and price; and (4) negotiating contract terms with successful bidders requires specialized personnel, is time consuming, and is costly. By effectively shifting this cost burden from vendors to hospitals (and, ultimately, their patients and payers), the bill would result in significant new direct costs for hospitals and indirect costs for patients and payers. For many hospitals, particularly small and rural hospitals, there may be no funds available to pay for these new direct costs.
- Second, because GPOs represent hundreds of hospitals and other health care organizations, they are able to negotiate better prices from a given vendor on a consistent basis than any individual hospital could obtain if acting on its own. If GPOs are eliminated, or their operations are substantially circumscribed—either of which could occur if the GPO Safe Harbor is eliminated—hospitals will be deprived of these significant price reductions.
- Third, as noted above, GPOs provide direct financial support to their hospitals. These funds are related to vendor fee income and substantially reduce overall hospital supply costs. The bill would eliminate this important source of cost savings for hospitals.
- Fourth, this bill would restrict the ability of the GPOs to negotiate on behalf of hospitals of various sizes, particularly small and rural hospitals, and to use their group purchasing power to obtain the lowest possible prices. GPOs, in aggregating volume, perform their legitimate functions which are to bring a wide range of benefits to the hospitals they serve. Eliminating the Safe Harbor provision would shift the entire burden of the purchasing process, distribution, patient safety and clinical evaluations solely on the backs of the hospitals, thereby threatening the financial health and even the existence of the hospitals. GPOs do not stand in the way of medical manufacturing companies having access to physicians or hospitals to present new technologies, innovations, and improvements.

* * *

In closing, we thank you for the opportunity to comment on the three proposed bills. We also thank you for your time at the hearing to listen to the progress that has been made by the HGPII. As the Subcommittee advised, the Initiative was created to encourage and sustain best ethical and business practices and to implement a process for monitoring and improving adherence to these practices. Already well underway, the Initiative must be supported, not burdened by new regulatory requirements that will drive up the cost of health care.

Todd Ebert
President, Amerinet

Charles E. Saunders, M.D.
Chairman and CEO, Broadlane

Don C. Black
President, Child Health Corporation of America

Darrel Weatherford
Chief Operating Officer, Consorta

Lee Perlman
President and CEO, GNYHA Ventures, Inc.

Jim Fitzgerald
President and CEO
HealthTrust Purchasing Group

Rand Ballard
Chief Operating Officer, MedAssets

Mark M. McKenna
President and CEO, Novation

Richard A. Norling
President and CEO, Premier Inc.

RIDDLE MEMORIAL HOSPITAL

March 21, 2006

The Honorable Arlen Specter
711 Hart Building
United States Senate
Washington, DC 20510

Dear Senator Specter:

As the President and CEO of Riddle Memorial Hospital, an independent, community Hospital in Media, Pennsylvania, I am writing to submit comments for the record for the Antitrust Subcommittee's March 15 hearing on hospital group purchasing organizations (GPOs). I appreciate the opportunity to voice my perspective on this important issue.

As hospitals are battling $100 billion in proposed cuts to the Medicare program, I am concerned that the Subcommittee is considering legislation that would place an additional $30 billion in costs on American hospitals and taxpayers.

My hospital is part of our community's health care safety net, and we also help anchor our local economy. In addition, we must stand ready to respond to natural disasters, pandemic diseases and the threat of terrorism. Now more than ever, we must do everything possible to control costs while improving care. One way we do this is by working with GPOs.

I don't think hospitals have been heard from often enough in this debate. Make no mistake, hospitals rely on GPOs.

- The two biggest costs for any hospital are salaries and supplies. Hospitals purchase about $200 billion worth of products and services annually through GPO contracts, about 72 percent of all purchases.
- Hospitals shave between 10-15 percent off supply costs when using a GPO.
- Hospital use of GPOs is on the rise. The latest independent survey shows a 17 percent increase in hospital usage between 2004 and 2005.
- Most hospitals belong to more than one GPO, and GPO membership grew by a six percent in 2005.

I was glad to hear that the Subcommittee heard from an Ohio hospital executive who stressed her organization's reliance on its GPO to help control costs while delivering the highest quality patient care. She also shared that her hospital purchases about 65 percent of medical supplies and devices through GPO contracts, and purchased the rest through direct vendor relationships. I want to assure you that this ratio is similar at my hospital and at hospitals across the country. The bottom line: hospitals make their own purchasing decisions based on a variety of factors, such as clinician preference and ease of conversion. Hospitals determine the best products; GPOs secure the best prices.

1068 West Baltimore Pike, Media, Pennsylvania 19063-5177 610-566-9400

Here at Riddle Memorial Hospital, we work with Novation, one of the leading health care GPOs. Over the last couple of years we have seen increased opportunities to purchase from small manufacturers and diverse suppliers, and working with Novation has helped us afford new and innovative technologies. We can do this because Novation negotiates discounted pricing on these new and important medical products.

Frankly, the arguments being offered against GPOs fail to acknowledge the real and positive progress the industry has made. I see GPOs competing vigorously in a dynamic marketplace, but also collaborating on industry transparency and ethics initiatives. I'm proud to say Novation was one of the founding members of the Healthcare Group Purchasing Industry Initiative. The Initiative was created to encourage and sustain best ethical and business practices and to implement a process for monitoring and improving adherence to these practices. Already well underway, the Initiative must be supported and unencumbered by regulatory burdens that will drive up the cost of health care.

Now is the wrong time to add additional and unnecessary costs to the nation's hospitals through GPO legislation.

Regards,

Dan Kennedy

Daniel E. Kennedy
President and CEO

Testimony of:

Mark B. Leahey, Esq.
Executive Director
Medical Device Manufacturers Association

Before the Subcommittee on Antitrust, Competition, and Business and Consumer Rights
of the U.S. Senate Judiciary Committee

"Hospital Group Purchasing: Are the Industry's Reforms Sufficient to Ensure Competition?"

March 15, 2006

The Medical Device Manufacturers Association (MDMA) is pleased to submit testimony to the Senate Judiciary Subcommittee on Antitrust, Competition, and Business and Consumer Rights concerning Group Purchasing Organizations' (GPOs) attempts to reform their anticompetitive practices. This is the fourth time that MDMA has submitted testimony for the record and I would encourage those interested to refer to our previous statements for more background on the issue.

MDMA is a national trade association representing the innovative and entrepreneurial sector of the medical device industry. We represent hundreds of makers of medical devices, diagnostic products, and health care information systems. MDMA seeks to improve the quality of patient care by encouraging the development of new medical technology and fostering the availability of innovative products in the marketplace.

Overview

The efforts of this Subcommittee, especially of Chairman DeWine and Senator Kohl, during the past four years have been important in highlighting ethical and contracting practices by the GPO industry that have negatively impacted the quality and cost of health care in this country. These practices have included multimillion dollar stock payments to GPO senior executives from companies they did business with, the receipt of stock options from companies seeking GPO contracts, and the charging of million dollar up-front payments from suppliers seeking preferential treatment. Additional contractual problems have included long-term and sole-source contracts, the bundling of unrelated products and from multiple favored companies, charging excessive fees, requiring participation in for-profit GPO business ventures and preventing physicians and caregivers from freely selecting the products they deem best for their patients. .

MDMA is grateful for the efforts of this Subcommittee and its dedicated staff in addressing these problems. However, the lack of resolve and commitment by the GPO industry has prevented widespread meaningful reforms from being enacted. While there has been success in eliminating the most egregious practices such as GPOs receiving stock options from contract seekers and personal investments by GPO leaders in supplier companies many serious problems still persist. It is readily apparent that after nearly four years of congressional oversight, the development of individual GPO codes of conduct, a GPO association code of conduct, and most recently the Healthcare Group Purchasing Industry Initiative ("GPO Initiative"), significant problems remain that are negatively impacting patients, caregivers, taxpayers, and innovation.

Since this process began in 2002, GPOs have not seemed to take the Subcommittee's requests for reform seriously. While GPOs publish codes and develop new "initiatives" that claim to have reformed the industry, their actions indicate otherwise. They continue to contract in exclusionary and anticompetitive ways, including bundling across companies and products, executing long-term contracts, engaging in sole-source contracts, awarding no-bid contracts, collecting excessive fees, and preventing caregivers and hospitals from access to a free and open marketplace of competitive products.

While MDMA would like nothing more than for the GPO industry to reform itself, that doesn't appear likely. Since the last hearing in October of 2004, additional press reports, private litigation and government investigations and reports continue to uncover anticompetitive and exclusionary practices, including the collection of excessive fees. For example, a recent antitrust case found that one supplier paid a single GPO $31 million in fees on a total of $345 million in business. This certainly exceeds the 3% fee that GPOs would have you believe they receive. If these payments exist between one vendor and one GPO, the broader impact of these fees is significant across the health care sector.

In 2005, the U.S. Department of Health and Human Services' Office of Inspector General published two audits examining the fees collected by 6 GPOs. The audits found that the 6 GPOs collected $2.3 billion in fees from vendors. Of that $2.3 billion, $1.6 billion exceeded their operating. Of the $1.6 billion, the GPOs withheld nearly $500 million from their member hospitals. Of the remaining funds the GPOs returned to their members, the majority of hospitals did not accurately reflect the fee receipts in their cost reports to Medicare.

Fortunately, a solution does exist that would restore competition in the health care marketplace, resulting in higher quality care at a lower cost. The answer is repealing the GPO "safe harbor" from the Medicare anti-kickback statute. This would end the financial dependence that GPOs have on a select group of dominant suppliers. This fee dependence is at the core of the anticompetitive and exclusionary practices of GPOs. So long as GPOs depend on fees from suppliers whose products they are charged with evaluating, patients will continue to be denied access to innovative, cost-effective technologies.

MDMA and our members understand and appreciate the rationale behind creating the GPO safe harbor in 1986. However, that exemption was established when there were hundreds of small, active GPOs and has never been modified despite the consolidation of GPOs to only seven having 85 % of the market with the two leading GPOs controlling over 60 % of the business. Clearly, the experiment has not worked as Congress had envisioned. As a result, MDMA urges this Subcommittee to introduce legislation that would still permit GPOs to continue to aggregate volume on behalf of their member hospitals, but would terminate the financial dependence that GPOs have on the vendor fees. Such legislation will help ensure that GPOs are promoting competition and innovation, while truly serving the best interests of their member hospitals, patients, and U.S. taxpayers.

Deficiencies with the Current GPO Initiative

In the spring of 2005, three years after GPOs created their own individual codes and two years after the HIGPA code was established, the GPOs created the Healthcare Group Purchasing Industry Initiative. The stated purpose of the Initiative was to monitor and promote best ethical and business practices. However, the Initiative permits each GPO to operate under their existing codes and it has no authority to prohibit anticompetitive practices. As a result, what real impact can the Initiative possibly have?

The GPO Initiative only has two requirements for their members. The first is that each member completes an annual questionnaire acknowledging that the GPO has created policies and procedures addressing certain issues. However, whether the underlying policies and procedures are meaningful or enforceable is irrelevant. Second, the GPO members must participate at an annual meeting with other GPOs. Nothing else is required. In addition, there is no real enforcement mechanism – the only penalty is being suspended from the Initiative itself.

This Initiative clearly is insufficient to address the ongoing exclusionary and anticompetitive practices of the GPO industry. As a result, action by this Subcommittee is necessary to ensure that patients, caregivers, and taxpayers are no longer harmed by GPO practices.

Repeal of the GPO "safe harbor" from the Medicare Anti-kickback Statute

So, what can be done? I strongly urge this Subcommittee, and Congress, to pursue the solution embodied in the "Ensuring Competition in Hospital Purchasing Act" draft bill circulated last fall. This proposal is the most efficient, effective option to reforming the GPOs' current anticompetitive practices. This repeal of the Medicare anti-kickback safe harbor would still permit the GPOs to aggregate volume on behalf of their member hospitals and thereby negotiate favorable prices for products and medical devices. All other efficiencies currently enjoyed by providers and suppliers would continue to exist. The only modification would be the GPOs' revenue source. Instead of continuing to be paid and influenced by their vendors, they once again would be compensated by their member hospitals. As a result, they clearly would need to show cost savings and value to justify their continued role as intermediaries negotiating with vendors.

Repealing the GPO safe harbor will undue a 20-year experiment that has obviously failed. The intention of the safe harbor was to create efficiencies and ensure that hospitals and patients have access to better products at a better price. However, based on various government reports and evidence presented during recent antitrust cases, this is not occurring. Unfortunately, under the current model, the GPOs seem more concerned about their fee revenues than with negotiating competitive contracts for their member hospitals.

Less Effective Alternatives

Other draft legislation has been proposed in an effort to help reform the anticompetitive practices of GPOs. While well-intended, these efforts create additional levels of bureaucracy and don't go far enough to truly reform the current system.

"The Medical Device Competition Act" is a draft proposal that would create additional contracting regulations, modify the existing safe harbor, create an independent certification process and establish penalties for non-compliance. However, there are concerns that this proposal may create another bureaucratic layer with unintended consequences. In addition, it creates additional demands on the Senate, the Federal Trade Commission and the Department of Health and Human Services to oversee the implementation of this process for years to come.

Another option, called "The Hospital Group Purchasing Organization Reform Act," may actually create a false sense of security. It also requires ongoing congressional oversight to ensure that the codes don't change and that no backsliding occurs. As the underlying codes have qualifying language limiting their effectiveness, it is very easy to certify compliance, yet no real reforms are likely.

Conclusion

In 2002, Senator Kohl said, "Without quick and effective self-regulation, we will have to consider congressional action." At that time, MDMA agreed with the Subcommittee's decision to allow time for a self-imposed code. The following year, Chairman DeWine stated, "our work in this area is not complete." It has been nearly four years since GPOs engaged in efforts to self reform and they have not achieved the results envisioned. As a result, legislative action is required to ensure that patients, caregivers, innovation and the American taxpayer have access to the best and safest products at the best prices.

I urge this Subcommittee to introduce legislation repealing the GPO safe harbor from the Medicare anti-kickback statute. It is vital to patient safety and to restoring competitive principles to the marketplace. Without a repeal of this safe harbor protection, patients and hospitals will continue to pay too much for medical devices and products – and will be denied access to the best and safest medical technology available today.

Thank you.

Mark Leahey
Executive Director
Medical Device Manufacturers Association

APPENDIX

The Current GPO Industry Initiative and Industry Code of Conduct Are Not Mandatory

In a letter dated September 2, 2004, to Chairman DeWine and Senator Kohl, former HIGPA President and CEO Robert Betz wrote that the HIGPA Code was "the only mandatory one in the health care supply chain." However, after a closer examination of the facts, one finds that this statement is incorrect. Multibillion dollar GPOs such as Broadlane, HealthTrust and others have not certified that they are in compliance with the HIGPA Code. In fact, they are not even members of HIGPA. As a result, the current Code is not mandatory within the industry.

Furthermore, the current Healthcare Group Purchasing Industry Initiative does not include all GPOs and is not mandatory across the entire GPO industry.

The Current GPO Initiative and Industry Code Have No "Teeth"

During the September 14, 2004, hearing, Chairman DeWine expressed concern that the self-policing codes did not have adequate penalties. In HIGPA's testimony to this Subcommittee submitted on July 16, 2003, Robert Betz said, "our Code of Conduct is the only Code in the health care industry that has a penalty for not complying with the principles, the penalty being, membership in the Association is revoked or denied." MDMA agrees with Chairman DeWine that the current penalties are not adequate. Losing your membership to a trade association is not an appropriate deterrent.

In addition to the industry code not having "teeth," Senator DeWine said, "most troubling is the fact that there is really no mechanism to discipline GPOs that don't follow their own code." MDMA agrees with this concern and it is valid with the GPO Initiative as well.

The GPO Initiative also fails to have any real penalties for non-compliance. GPOs *may* be suspended from the GPO Initiative for failure to meet the basic requirements of responding to a questionnaire and attending an annual meeting. However, even if a GPO fails to meet these minimal standards, the impact of being suspended from an organization that was established less than a year ago and has no real purpose is questionable.

Concerns of Backsliding with the Current GPO Initiative and Industry Code

During the hearings, both Senators DeWine and Kohl expressed concern about backsliding. MDMA shares their concerns about this as well. In fact, MDMA has already witnessed backsliding from certain GPOs. The third largest GPO amended its code less than seven months after enactment. The amended code eliminated language prohibiting certain types of bundling and other anticompetitive contracting practices.

In HIGPA's July 16, 2003, testimony before this Subcommittee, Betz said the Code was a "living document." GPOs have made the same claims about their individual codes. MDMA is concerned that without repealing the GPO "safe harbor" from the Medicare anti-kickback statute, problems will persist and these so-called living documents will revert back to old practices, even in areas where GPOs have shown modest improvements.

Eliminating the GPO safe harbor from the Medicare anti-kickback statute would provide the most effective and efficient solution to the exclusionary and anti-competitive practices of the GPO industry. In addition, it would not require ongoing congressional oversight.

Fear of Retribution

Without eliminating the GPO safe harbor – which would result in free and open markets in health care – manufactures, health care workers and others, face severe retribution. During the September 2004 hearing, Joe Kiani, CEO of Masimo, testified that he was the target of retribution from a multibillion dollar GPO because of his efforts to reform the GPO marketplace. The email Mr. Kiani cited at the September 2004 hearing was from a GPO CEO and stated that he (Kiani) was "either with us or against us. I will know by your support of this legislation" (referring to a California bill seeking to provide greater oversight of the GPO industry). Mr. Kiani continued to push for reforms. Shortly thereafter, Masimo's contract with HealthTrust was terminated and the GPO entered into a sole-source agreement with Tyco for pulse oximeters. It is worth noting that HealthTrust awarded Masimo a contract before any of the GPO investigations began and only terminated the contract once Mr. Kiani came forward to address the exclusionary and anticompetitive practices of the GPO industry.

This type of retribution will be commonplace unless real and lasting reform occurs. This can be achieved by repealing the GPO safe harbor from the Medicare anti-kickback statute.

The GPO Initiative is Dependent on Inconsistent and Ambiguous Codes

The GPO Initiative is entirely dependent on GPO self certification that they are in compliance with their own code of conduct. However, on July 16, 2003, the GAO published a report on the GPOs' codes of conduct. The GAO found, ***"the conduct codes are not uniform in how they address business practices. In addition, some GPOs' conduct codes include exceptions and qualified language that could limit their potential to effect change."*** Therefore, certifying compliance to codes that have no teeth is not proof that the GPOs have reformed. In fact, it merely provides a false sense of security that things have changed.

The examples below indicate that little has changed related to the exclusionary and anticompetitive practices of GPOs.

Specific Examples of Continued Anticompetitive Behavior from Certain GPOs

- Hospitals and Clinicians Lack Choice
  GPOs and incumbent vendors still may prevent a hospital or clinicians from selecting alternative products they deem necessary. Certain GPOs still require their approval as well as the incumbent vendor's approval before a hospital can purchase a competitor's product off contract. This allows the dominant supplier incredible leverage over their competitors.

- Bundling of Companies
  Two of the three market-leading GPOs continue to promote programs that bundle companies. These programs artificially tie the success or failure of one company with that of another. This practice excludes other manufacturers who are not part of the exclusive bundle from gaining access to the marketplace. Until recently, little was known about what suppliers paid to be part of the bundle. Recent evidence in an antitrust case showed that fees were 5%. This highlights the problem that a select group of vendors enjoy preferential treatment if they pay the GPO significant fees.

- Bundling of Unrelated Products
  GPOs continue to solicit bids that bundle unrelated, clinical-preference products. In many cases, the GPOs have posted or solicited bids that bundle unrelated products that only one or two vendors could supply. This excludes smaller, more efficient competitors from participating in the bid process simply because they lack product breadth.

- Inviting Bundled Bids
  Although GPOs have said that they will break up product bundles and bid contracts based on individual product categories, they are still asking vendors to submit two different pricing schemes: one price for a bundled contract, the other for individual products. The end result is often a bundled contract.

- High Commitment Levels
  Two of the three largest GPOs continue to promote programs that require their hospitals to purchase between 90-95% of a particular product from one supplier. In addition, in order to receive the rebates, compliance must exceed 90-95% across multiple product categories. These types of programs prevent hospitals from being able to choose alternative products that are clinically preferred or more cost-effective because they will forfeit their rebates unless they meet the high thresholds.

- Requiring Participation in Other Business Ventures
  While the days of million dollar payoffs for "Innovation Councils" may be behind us (or postponed), Novation, the market-leading GPO, continues to pressure manufacturers to sign up for Neoforma, a separate e-commerce company, as a prerequisite to being awarded a contract. This is required even if a supplier has no intention or the capabilities of selling their product through an e-commerce platform. In addition, Novation requires the supplier to negotiate in good faith with Neoforma for the purchase of additional supply chain solutions. One must remember that the owners of Novation also own Neoforma.

- Private Label Programs
  Two GPOs, including the market leader, continue to engage in the practice of private labeling and receive excessive fees for this practice. Private labeling is a tactic used by some GPOs to collect money outside the "administrative fee" structure since it is not closely monitored. These fees far exceed the recommended 3% administrative fee and are collected on top of the administrative fee.

- Excessive Fees
  The nation's largest GPO will not cap administrative fees on non-clinical preference items at 3%. This provides the opportunity for a supplier to pay the 3% maximum for clinical preference products, but pay as much as the GPO wants to charge for the non-clinical products. A supplier who is only willing to pay 3% for both product categories will likely lose out on the contract, regardless of the quality or the price of the product.

  In 1991, the OIG noted that the legislative history of the 1987 law "shows Congress's concern for excessive GPO fees, particularly those exceeding 3 percent," and thereby revised the rule to require a GPO to specify the administrative fee "only if any fee will be above 3 percent." The OIG believed that this would "retain the focus on excessive fees about which Congress was concerned." [56 Federal Register 35952, 35982]

  Today, GPOs are no longer using the safe harbor simply as a means to cover the costs of contracting as Congress intended. In fact, contracts that had previously charged 2% admin fees are now charging 3% for renewals. These new contracts do not even require additional product evaluations. They are simply extensions of existing contracts, yet they charge a higher fee. This type of behavior only adds baseless costs to the overall health care marketplace.

- GPOs Not Acting in the Best Interest of Their Members
  During the September 2004 hearing, evidence was presented showing that the market-leading GPO actively sought to recommit its hospital members to the incumbent vendor over a smaller vendor. However, both suppliers had a GPO contract. This contradicts what GPOs say about being "neutral middleman." In addition, the solicitation to recommit needed to be executed by October 31, 2003.

What the GPO failed to disclose to its member hospitals was the fact that two weeks later, a cheaper generic version would be available at a minimum of 30% savings.

This is not surprising since the current system rewards the GPO for contracting for the higher priced product, because its fees are based on a percentage of the total contract price. If the member hospital contracted for the less expensive product, the GPOs revenues would have decreased 30%. This example illustrates the fact that the member hospitals of a GPO often do not have all the information they need to make an informed decision. Repealing the GPO safe harbor from the Medicare anti-kickback statute would ensure that the GPOs aggressively negotiated on behalf of their member companies and were responsible solely for their member hospitals.

- Back to Sole Sourcing (Second Event Program)
  On December 16, 2003, at a GPOs' supplier meeting in Chicago, IL, GPO executives discussed a "second event" program. This entails the GPO contracting with multiple vendors for clinical preference items on a national level so they would comply with their code of conduct and the Senate's request for multi-sourcing. However, the GPO would then permit a "second event," which would be a sole-source contract at the regional or IDN level. The GPO would collect the admin fee on this sole-source second event as well. This is being done by MANY GPOs. While this may meet the letter of the codes, it certainly falls short of the spirit or intent.

Statement of Senator Patrick Leahy
Antitrust Subcommittee of the Judiciary Committee
"Hospital Group Purchasing:
Are The Industry's Reforms Sufficient To Ensure Competition?"
March 15, 2006

It is no secret that the health care system in America is in crisis. Each year more Americans fall into the ranks of the uninsured, and even for those who can afford insurance, health care costs are rising relentlessly. These costs place a significant strain on the pocketbooks of all Americans, and as a society – and as a government – we must make real efforts to contain them.

The problem of rising health care costs is compounded by the correlation often seen between the quality of health care and the cost of health care. This relationship makes the fight to keep health care costs down, while simultaneously ensuring first-rate care, an arduous task. Hospital group purchasing organizations, or GPOs, were developed as one part of a possible solution to this clear and pressing concern.

The idea behind GPOs is to allow hospitals to aggregate their buying power by purchasing all their medical supplies and equipment from purchasing groups. Because purchasing groups buy in bulk and handle the administrative tasks dealing with suppliers, hospitals save substantial amounts of money and time. In other words, GPOs were created to provide a better solution to the cost versus quality conundrum—hospitals could effectively cut costs without having to sacrifice quality service.

Within recent years, however, public and industry commentary have indicated there are some important issues that should be addressed in the context of GPO operations. This Subcommittee has held several hearings to address these concerns and, because of Senators Kohl and DeWine's leadership, the GPOs have established a voluntary ethical "code of conduct." I commend this effort, and any such effort to further the goals of efficient and effective health care.

We come together again today to revisit the issue in the wake of recent criticism that these steps are insufficient. We know our bottom line is to provide all Americans with health care that is affordable, first-rate in quality, and technologically advanced. These goals are intimately related—ensuring that new companies and technologies have access to the marketplace will fuel competition, which will help guarantee that patients have the best possible health care at the lowest possible price.

It is time that we in Congress decide what legislation, if any, should be introduced in order to bring us closer to our bottom line. I understand that the problems of the health care system do not lend themselves to quick and easy fixes. However, I am confident that under the responsible leadership of Senator Kohl and Senator DeWine we can find the right answers, sooner rather than later.

# # # # #

The Honorable Mike DeWine, Chairman
Senate Subcommittee on Antitrust, Competition
Policy and Consumer Rights
140 Russell Senate Office Building
Washington, DC 20510

The Honorable Herb Kohl, Ranking Member
Senate Subcommittee on Antitrust, Competition
Policy and Consumer Rights
330 Hart Senate Office Building
Washington, DC 20510

March 29, 2006

Dear Senators DeWine and Kohl:

As Chairman of the Health Group Purchasing Association (HIGPA), I am writing to you in strong support of the attached testimony submitted by the nine CEOs that founded the Healthcare Group Purchasing Industry Initiative (HGPII). Together, we are responding to your letter of March 15, 2006, requesting comment on three draft bills relating to hospital group purchasing organizations ("GPOs"): (1) the "Medical Device Competition Act" ("S.2880"); (2) the "Hospital Group Purchasing Organization Reform Act"; and (3) the "Ensuring Competition in Hospital Purchasing Act."

The original claim put forth by the Medical Device Manufacturers Association, which represents small manufacturers in the medical device industry, that initiated the March 15 hearing was that GPOs block access of new and innovative technologies to hospitals, physicians, caregivers and, ultimately, patients. The Subcommittee has now heard testimony and received endorsements from many individual hospitals, the Ohio Hospital Association, the Wisconsin Hospital Association and other related institutions—all affirming that GPOs in no way pose barriers to such access. Nothing impedes a hospital's ability to purchase the products and technologies that the hospital and its medical staff need to deliver high quality patient care. Furthermore, nothing impedes a small manufacturing company from approaching any hospital, physician or provider with a new technology or product innovation.

The most important point in response to the question at hand is that hospitals have had and will continue to have the power to make every decision regarding what is in the best interest of their facilities, medical staff and patients. This issue has been fully reviewed in recent years by the Federal Trade Commission and the Department of Justice as well as other federal and state regulatory agencies. All have concluded that the role of the GPO is appropriate and provides a great value to the U.S. health system.

In the joint comments being submitted to you today, I believe you will find additional evidence in our overwhelming and compelling case against additional governmental regulation of the relationship between hospitals and their GPOs. Every day, hospitals face daunting challenges in how to control costs while improving the care provided to patients. GPOs are an essential tool that hospitals rely on to provide unlimited care on a limited budget. The three legislative proposals we were asked to review would severely limit, if not eliminate altogether, the ability of hospitals to work with GPOs, particularly small and rural hospitals. Hospitals would be unable to leverage the GPO purchasing power that enables them to afford the essential but expensive equipment and supplies they need. In this way, these proposed bills do not assist in delivering improved health care.

These bills would also increase the costs of medical care, namely within the health care supply chain delivery stream, that would, in part, be passed on to patients and payers, including taxpayer-funded programs via the federal government. The written testimony before you presents evidence from a recent study by Muse & Associates estimating that an earlier version of these legislative proposals, contained in S. 2880, could increase total direct U.S. health care spending by between $23.9 billion and $34.6 billion over ten years and increase the cost to Medicare and Medicaid by between $8.2 billion and $9.7 billion over the same ten year period. These increased expenses and burdensome regulations would undoubtedly fall most heavily on small and rural hospitals.

However, all hospitals will directly suffer from the overly-regulated approach to group purchasing that would result from the bureaucracy these bills create. A one-size-fits-all GPO framework would stifle today's highly competitive environment that encourages innovative solutions and creative efforts to further increase savings and improve clinical outcomes. In effect, these proposed legislative regulations would inhibit all hospitals' ability to guarantee the highest quality of care for patients.

GPOs exist to help hospitals improve patient care and control health care costs – and GPOs are doing it with greater transparency than ever before. GPOs provide procurement vehicles empowering hospitals to purchase medical equipment and supplies at substantially reduced group rates. In addition to these direct savings, GPOs relieve hospitals of the costs of staffing for acquisition planning, market research, and purchasing. At the same time, hospitals remain free to purchase directly from manufacturers or to use GPOs, thus promoting competition. Vendors who choose to sell through GPOs are able to capitalize on volume and on being relieved of some costs related to marketing and selling. As was presented to the Subcommittee in our testimony at the March 15 hearing, both the GPO industry, through HGPII, and individual GPOs, have established—and are implementing—detailed codes of conduct that address the principal concerns raised both by the Subcommittee and other interested parties. The HGPII now underlies the above process by assuring the public interest in transparency and accountability for ethical business practices. These new practices protect hospitals, particularly small and rural medical facilities, and the industry program will oversee and assure adherence to the rigorous codes of conduct and an annual cycle of public reporting and accountability.

We firmly believe that the voluntary approach represented by HGPII is the best way to promote and monitor best ethical and business practices. Truly, the Initiative is an effort that works on behalf of hospitals and the highest quality of care for patients. Already well underway, the Initiative must be given an opportunity to be fully implemented to achieve its mission, rather than burdening hospitals with new regulations that will drive up the cost of health care.

While specific comments on each proposal are included in the testimony, please note that the GPO industry is serious in its efforts to create a workable self-regulatory framework that will function in the best interests of hospitals and the patients they serve. It is appropriate that the Senate give this serious initiative a chance to work.

At the March 15 hearing, we had hoped to provide data that assesses the attitudes of hospitals toward the performance of GPOs and the level of satisfaction hospitals feel toward their GPOs. This study is taking longer to complete than we had anticipated. We respectfully request that the Subcommittee extend the comment and submission period to include this information as soon as it becomes available.

In closing, thank you for the opportunity to submit these comments for the record and for your consideration of our request that the comment and submission be extended to allow for any additional supporting information we are able to provide.

Sincerely,

Al LoBiondo
Chairman
Health Industry Group Purchasing Association

Novation®

125 E. John Carpenter Freeway
Irving, TX 75602-2324
888/7-NOVATE • novationco.com

The Honorable Mike DeWine, Chairman
Senate Subcommittee on Antitrust, Competition
Policy and Consumer Rights
140 Senate Russell Office Building
Washington, D.C. 20510

The Honorable Herb Kohl, Ranking Member
Senate Subcommittee on Antitrust, Competition
Policy and Consumer Rights
330 Senate Hart Office Building
Washington, D.C. 20510

Dear Senator DeWine and Senator Kohl:

Novation has joined other GPOs and sent a letter responding to the subcommittee's request for comments on various draft legislative proposals that would impose additional government regulation on GPOs or revoke the current GPO exception in the Anti-Kickback statute. We will not repeat our views on proposed legislation in this letter. The purpose of this letter is to add one additional point about the legislation and correct the record concerning numerous misstatements in the testimony presented to the subcommittee on March 15, 2006 by Mr. Mark Leahey, Executive Director of the Medical Device Manufacturers Association. Mr. Leahey made sweeping accusations about GPO industry-wide misconduct. We want to ensure that the subcommittee record reflects an accurate description of Novation's business practices. This letter will also address the mischaracterizations concerning competitiveness in the GPO industry contained in the testimony of Dr S. Prakesh Sethi.

Novation

Novation is a health care contracting services company that is jointly owned by VHA Inc. and the University HealthSystem Consortium (UHC). VHA is a health care cooperative comprised of more than 2,800 not-for-profit hospitals and health care organizations. UHC is a cooperative that is owned and governed by 93 academic medical center members, and it has an additional 137 associate members. GPOs like Novation utilize the combined purchasing power of participating members to obtain lower prices for life-saving medical supplies, drugs and devices. GPOs also help member hospitals avoid significant costs associated with procuring products and services by providing centralized procurement services and expert personnel at minimal cost to individual members. Suppliers willingly compensate GPOs for the value they receive: aggregated volume, reduced sales costs and increased overall contracting efficiencies. The cornerstones of Novation's offering are its market-leading contract portfolio, the best prices, and hospital choice.

I. Additional Point About Arbitrary Fee Cap

Two of the proposed options, S. 2880 and the Hospital Group Purchasing Reform Act, provide for a three percent cap on administrative fees. Novation believes such a cap not only is arbitrary, it also is unnecessary and counterproductive. It is unnecessary because the existing GPO Safe Harbor provides for complete transparency between GPOs and their hospital members with respect to fees that exceed three percent. The provision is counterproductive because many GPOs make quarterly or annual distributions to their members. These distributions — which effectively (and substantially) reduce overall hospital supply costs — necessarily will be reduced if administrative fees are arbitrarily capped at three percent.

II. Leahey Testimony

Background

At the outset, we note that some of the inaccurate assertions made by Mr. Leahey at the recent hearing were distortions that were in his testimony to the subcommittee in 2004. Novation offered comments in 2004 to correct that record, as well. Examples cited in Mr. Leahey's recent testimony pre-date Novation's adoption of its Code of Conduct and Operating Principles on August 8, 2002. It is a sign that industry reforms have worked that Mr. Leahey did not have a single new example of alleged exclusion of innovative technology. Also, as noted by Senator Schumer during the March 15 hearing, Mr. Leahey, in his role as Executive Director of a supplier trade association, is not a convincing advocate for devising ways to lower the prices paid by hospitals to MDMA members.

Points of Clarification

1. Adequacy of GPO Industry Initiative.

Novation was one of the founding members of the Healthcare Group Purchasing Industry Initiative (HGPII). The Initiative was created to encourage and sustain best ethical and business practices and to implement a process for monitoring and improving adherence to these practices. Already well underway, the Initiative has completed a full cycle of public disclosure of business practices by the nine GPOs, including Novation, and has held its first annual Best Practices Seminar, in which Novation participated.

2. Adequacy of Individual GPO Codes of Conduct.

Novation adopted a rigorous Code of Conduct and Operating Principles on August 8, 2002. The Code of Conduct is not transitory; it has become part of the internal fabric of the company. Code requirements are included in all aspects of Novation's operations, including training, product evaluation and contracting. The Compliance Officer responsible for enforcement of the Code of Conduct is in the top tier of Novation's management team. As part of its Code of Conduct, Novation has:

- Increased its focus on identifying new and innovative technology and, since August 2002, has awarded 50 agreements to innovative technology companies for their products. These contracts generated more than $50 million in sales for these companies in 2005.

- Created a Technology Forum web site that can be used by small companies to post information about their products that can be viewed by Novation customers, regardless of whether the firms have agreements with Novation.

- Established a formal grievance process that enables manufacturers that did not win a contract through the public competitive bid process to request reconsideration by Novation member councils.

- Reduced the number of single-source agreements it signs for clinical preference products and has moved towards dual- and multi-source arrangements for almost all of these types of products. For example, in 2004, Novation awarded 17 separate contracts to six different suppliers for wound closure and endomechanical products, a category that had typically been contracted as one award by the industry.

- Eliminated its OPPORTUNITY® and Spectrum commitment programs, and reduced commitment levels for its voluntary standardization purchasing programs.

- Focused its private label program, NOVAPLUS®, exclusively on commodity products.

- Reduced vendor fees to three percent or less for all products identified as clinical preference items.

- Appointed a compliance officer who is accountable to the board of directors. This individual ensures adherence to the commitments that were made to the Senate Subcommittee.

2. Level of Choice Enjoyed by Hospitals and Clinicians.

Hospitals that participate in Novation are free to purchase on or off contract. In fact, VHA and UHC members purchase nearly 40% of their products outside of Novation contracts. Hospital members are free to participate in Novation's Standardization Program, where the hospital, for health and safety reasons, chooses to buy certain products from a small number of suppliers. Standardization maximizes consistency of performance and interoperability, and reduces training costs. Novation does not require hospitals to obtain approval from Novation or any vendor before a hospital can purchase a competitor's product off-contract.

3. Bundling of Companies

Novation does not promote programs that include a bundle of products from a single company. In fact, it has rejected supplier-proposed bundles that often include marketing leading products with a mixture of other products.

4. Bundling of Unrelated Products

Novation does not solicit or accept bids that bundle unrelated product categories.

5. High Commitment Levels

Novation offers a standardization program that covers clinical preference and commodity products. Some members choose to participate in the program because of the benefits of product consistency and availability. For clinical preference products, the added benefits of interoperability make it less expensive to train staff on the use of multiple versions of sophisticated medical devices. Participation in standardization programs is strictly voluntary, and commitment levels do not exceed 90%. All Novation contracts may be terminated without cause, upon 90 days written notice.

6. Vendor Participation in Other GPO Business Ventures

In March 2006, Neoforma, an e-commerce company, was purchased by GHX, a technology company owned in part by suppliers. Novation never required manufacturers to sign-up for Neoforma as a prerequisite to being awarded a Novation contract. However, VHA and UHC member made it clear to Novation that they preferred to do business with companies that were ready to do business on the Web, and this impacted Novation council decisions about contract awards.

7. Private Label Programs

Novation's private label program, NOVAPLUS®, includes only commodity products and offers hospitals the opportunity to obtain significant savings on basic products used in patient care, such as exam gloves, plastic basins and alcohol wipes, and on products not related to patient care, such as office supplies and floor wax. For NOVAPLUS products, Novation provides marketing and promotional support, as well as licensing arrangements. The suppliers pay Novation for these added services as part of the administrative fee for the contract. Even so, the average administrative fee for all Novation contracts is 2%.

8. Fees.

Novation Operating Principles include a 3% cap on administrative fees for clinical preference products. However, the administrative fees play no role in the selection of products for Novation contracts. In fact, Novation's member-driven clinical councils and task forces have no visibility to the proposed supplier fees when they are making contract award recommendations. Contract awards are determined by 37 specialty councils and task forces comprised of 300 clinicians and material managers drawn from more than 180 VHA and UHC member organizations throughout the country. Low-best bidders are awarded based on member-determined criteria that measure both financial (price) and non-financial criteria, such as quality, ability to fulfill and ease of conversion. It is not Novation's practice to raise fees on contract extensions. Actually, all clinical preference products go through a technology review before these contracts can be extended.

In his testimony, Mark Leahey asserts that a recent antitrust case found that one supplier paid a single GPO $31 million in fees on a total of $345 million in business. Leahey was quoted in the media as identifying the supplier as Tyco and the GPO as Novation. This relates to a Tyco document presented as an exhibit in an antitrust matter, as Mr. Leahey states. Novation was not a party to this matter, which was tried in 2003. However, we do know that these sales and revenue numbers relate to Tyco contracts that covered 25 different product categories, not a single product category, as he implied. Nearly half of the $31 million that Mr. Leahey characterizes as Novation administrative fee revenue was in fact funds that were rebated directly to the hospital members. These funds cannot be called administrative fees.

9. Best Interest of GPO Members

Hospitals make purchases through GPOs to get the best products and services at the lowest price. Hospitals are sophisticated consumers – many hospitals that participate in Novation belong to at least one other GPO. Novation's operations are transparent to its members, which have 24 hour/365 day Internet access to "up-front" notice of vendor contract administrative fee provisions. Under Novation's management compensation system, employee bonuses increase as overall supply costs for its hospital member's decrease.

In his testimony, Mr. Leahy repeated an old example that was mischaracterized at the 2004 Senate Subcommittee hearing on hospital group purchasing – and Novation corrected that point in the record at that time. Leahey purports that a memo was sent to Novation customers in 2003 encouraging them to recommit to an incumbent vendor over a smaller vendor. As a standard practice, Novation communicates with members when new products are available under contract. The purpose and the intent of the memo was to make member hospitals aware of programmatic changes, including the opportunity to reduce commitment levels if desired, the availability of a new product under contract, and to reinforce that member hospitals can purchase products from any supplier. Management of the small supplier reviewed the letter before signing off on their agreement with Novation, yet it was again offered at a hearing as an example of egregious behavior by Novation.

10. Single Sourcing

The majority of Novation's contracts are dual-source or multi-source. Since implementing its Operating Principles, Novation has made great strides in reducing the number of sole-source contracts. In fact, Novation enters into a sole-source contract only when one of its member Councils or Task Forces determines that such an agreement would provide substantial value without compromising patient care. However, any member hospital may request assistance from Novation in negotiating a custom contract with a single supplier. But, the broader choice still would exist for other members. All Novation contracts may be terminated without cause, upon 90 days written notice.

III. Sethi Testimony

In his testimony, Dr. Sethi proposes to determine whether HGPII "will be sufficient to ensure competition in the health care supply industry." He has indicated that he will provide support for his comments in a forthcoming report being prepared by the International Center for Corporate Accountability (ICCA). We request the opportunity to comment on that report at the appropriate time.

In his testimony before the subcommittee on March 15, Dr. Sethi's criticizes the GPO's receipt of vendor fees. He claims that this practice gives the GPOs an incentive to favor large suppliers at the expense of smaller rivals and new entrants.

Dr. Sethi does not explain, however, why the payment of vendor fees *under the conditions specified in the GPOs' codes of conduct* creates the conditions under which anticompetitive contracts (presumably the "illegality" he identifies) can flourish. By his indiscriminate use of the term "anticompetitive contractual arrangements," Dr. Sethi fails to account for the structural reforms that have ensured that multiple bidders can participate and that GPOs will often choose multiple contracting partners. These are not the conditions that support the making of anticompetitive contracts.

Conclusion

U.S. hospitals and their patients derive important benefits from group purchasing organizations. Efforts by special interests to undermine the business operations of GPOs will result in higher health care costs for all Americans. Congress should proceed with caution in considering possible additional restrictions on GPO practices. Such intervention is not justified absent very clear evidence that GPO practices are resulting in anticompetitive effects, not just lost sales to particular competitors. The better course for Congress is to allow the significant competition that exists in the GPO marketplace to continue to evolve and to observe the implementation of HGPII, the new industry initiative.

Regards,

Mark McKenna

Mark McKenna

President and CEO

Novation

OhioHealth

David P. Blom
1087 Dennison Avenue
Columbus, Ohio 43201-3201
614 | 544-5430 fax | 544-5244
www.ohiohealth.com

March 22, 2006

The Honorable Mike DeWine
140 Russell Senate Building
United States Senate
Washington, DC 20510

Dear Senator DeWine:

On behalf of OhioHealth, I am writing to submit comments for the record for the Antitrust Subcommittee's March 15th hearing on hospital group purchasing organizations (GPOs). We appreciate the opportunity to voice our perspective on this important issue.

As hospitals are battling $100 billion in proposed cuts to the Medicare program, I am concerned that the Subcommittee is considering legislation that would place an additional $30 billion in costs on American hospitals and taxpayers.

Our health system is part of our community's health care safety net, and we also help anchor our local economy. In addition, we must stand ready to respond to natural disasters, pandemic diseases and the threat of terrorism. Now more than ever, we must do everything possible to control costs while improving care and one way we do this is by working with GPOs.

I was glad to hear that the Subcommittee heard from an Ohio hospital executive, Mina Ubbing, who stressed her organization's reliance on its GPO to help control costs while delivering the highest quality patient care. She also shared that her hospital purchases about 65 percent of medical supplies and devices through GPO contracts, and purchased the rest through direct vendor relationships. I want to assure you that this ratio is similar at our hospitals and at hospitals across the country. The bottom line: hospitals make their own purchasing decisions based on a variety of factors, such as clinician preference and ease of conversion. Hospitals determine the best products; GPOs secure the best prices.

The Healthcare Group Purchasing Industry Initiative was created to encourage and sustain best ethical and business practices and to implement a process for monitoring and improving adherence to these practices. Already well underway, the Initiative should be supported and unencumbered by any such regulatory burdens that will drive up the cost of health care. Thank you for your interest and attention to this matter.

Sincerely,

David P. Blom
President and Chief Executive Officer

PREMIER

• 12225 EL CAMINO REAL
SAN DIEGO, CA 92130
• T 858 481 2727
F 858 481 8919

• 2320 CASCADE POINTE BLVD (28208)
P.O. BOX 668800
CHARLOTTE, NC 28266-8800
• T 704 357 0022
F 704 357 6611

• 700 COMMERCE DRIVE
SUITE 100
OAK BROOK, IL 60523
• T 630 891 4100
F 630 368 5310

• 444 N CAPITOL STREET NW
SUITE 625
WASHINGTON, DC 20001-1511
• T 202 393 0860
F 202 393 6499

PREMIERINC.COM

March 29, 2006

The Honorable Mike DeWine, Chairman
Senate Subcommittee on Antitrust, Competition
Policy and Consumer Rights
140 Russell Senate Office Building
Washington, DC 20510

The Honorable Herb Kohl, Ranking Member
Senate Subcommittee on Antitrust, Competition
Policy and Consumer Rights
330 Hart Senate Office Building
Washington, DC 20510

Dear Senators DeWine and Kohl:

At the hearing of the Senate Subcommittee on Antitrust, Competition Policy and Consumer Rights on Wednesday, March 15, 2006, the executive director of the Medical Device Manufacturers Association, Mark Leahey, held up a sharps device (needle and syringe) and made comments about Premier Inc. We are writing to clarify several facts.

Mr. Leahey's comments do not appear in his written testimony, but it seemed to those present that he was implying that:

1. Premier has sharps devices on contract that cost more than devices available from non-contracted suppliers.
2. Premier does not inform its members of these less expensive sharps devices.

To the extent that this accurately reflects what Mr. Leahey said, both comments reflect a basic misunderstanding of the way Premier operates.

1. We are an alliance owned by not-for-profit hospitals. Our member hospitals *tell us* what products they want on contract based on numerous product-specific performance criteria and characteristics, of which cost is only one factor.

   On our publicly accessible Safety Institute Web site we provide our members and the public with a list of the more than 20 suppliers under contract with Premier, but also access to comprehensive list of all sharps/needle safety products on the market. (http://www.premierinc.com/all/safety/resources/needlestick/sharps-lists.jsp) Our goal is to assure our members are aware of all products on the market to meet the intent of the Needlestick Safety and Prevention Act, to have frontline workers select the products.

PREMIER

2. Through our member contracting committees, *our member hospitals* evaluate the pricing and features offered by suppliers and then elect which suppliers to offer contracts.

   The idea that Premier could somehow control information about non-contracted products runs contrary to our alliance model and basic market dynamics; pricing information flows from the purchasers - our member hospitals - to us, not the other way around.

If a member hospital wants to use a non-contracted product because it's less expensive, they are free to do so without penalty or repercussions. We specifically state on our public Safety Web site: "These (sharps safety device) contracts offer a cost-effective selection of devices for evaluation. Please note, however, that all safety devices the organization's staff considers appropriate should be evaluated, whether or not they are covered by a group contract."

Our member hospitals would not remain with Premier for long if our contracted prices were routinely higher than the prices for equivalent non-contracted products or if we were contracting for products other than the ones they want to use.

Finally, Mr. Leahey's comments may have given the impression that Premier has only one sharps safety device on contract. In fact, we have a wide variety of companies and products on contract, as reflected in the listing below:

Procedure needles	Cardinal Health
Procedure needles	Medical Device Technologies, Inc.
Safety phlebotomy products (includes safety phlebotomy device, safety winged steel needle device, and safety lancets)	Becton Dickinson
Safety phlebotomy products (includes safety phlebotomy device & safety winged steel needle device)	ICU Medical, Inc.
Safety phlebotomy products (includes safety phlebotomy device, safety winged steel needle device, and safety lancets)	Smith's Medical (Portex).
Safety phlebotomy product - safety lancets	International Technidyne Corp (ITC)
Safety phlebotomy products (includes safety phlebotomy device)	Retractable Technologies Inc (RTI)
Needleless IV access devices	Alaris Medical Systems
Needleless IV access devices	Baxter Healthcare Becton Dickinson
Needleless IV access devices	Tyco
Huber safety needle	Smiths Medical MD Inc (fka

PREMIER

	Deltec)
Huber safety needle	MPS Acacia
Huberloc (Huber needle remover)	Baxter
Safety Introducer for Percutaneous Endoscopic Gastrostomy (PEG) feeding tube (part of insertion kit)	Bard
Safety IV catheters	Becton Dickinson
Safety IV catheters	B. Braun USA
Safety IV catheters	Medex
Safety hypodermic/syringes	Becton Dickinson
Safety hypodermic/syringes	Retractable Technologies Inc- (RTI)
Safety hypodermic/syringes	Smith's Medical (Portex)
Safety hypodermic/syringes	Tyco

We welcome the opportunity to provide any additional information that might help to clarify this topic.

Sincerely,

Susan D. DeVore

Susan D. DeVore
President, Premier Purchasing Partners

Statement of

Thomas J. Shaw, President & CEO

Retractable Technologies, Inc.

Before the

United States Senate

Committee on the Judiciary

Subcommittee on Antitrust, Competition Policy, and Consumer Rights

Hearing on

"Hospital Group Purchasing:

Are the Industry's Reforms Sufficient to Ensure Competition?"

March 15, 2006

Once again, on behalf of my colleagues at Retractable Technologies and other small medical device makers, I'd like to thank you, the Members and staff of this Subcommittee, particularly Senators DeWine and Kohl, for your hard work and determination to halt the abuses of the giant hospital group purchasing organizations and their big supplier partners, and to remove the barriers to free market competition in the medical device industry. I'm told that holding a fourth hearing in as many years on an issue of this kind is a rare occurrence in Washington. You could have easily held a couple of hearings, issued a few press releases, declared victory and moved on to the next topic. Instead, you stuck with a difficult, arcane and not especially glamorous issue over several years, listening patiently to testimony, poring over documents, weighing evidence, and most recently, drafting corrective legislation. I greatly appreciate the opportunity to work with you on a solution to this problem, and I hope that America's patients, healthcare workers, and taxpayers will soon be able to reap the benefits of your good work through passage of your bill to repeal the Medicare/Medicaid anti-kickback safe harbor.

Investigations by this Subcommittee and *The New York Times* have exposed myriad conflicts of interest and violations of antitrust law, including tying and bundling and exclusionary long-term, sole source contracting practices, and payments of bribes and kickbacks by vendors to the GPOs. In turn, your inquiry has spawned probes by other federal and state agencies. Studies by the General Accountability Office have challenged GPO claims that they save hospitals money, and recent reports by the Office of Inspector General of the Department of Health and Human Services demonstrated that the GPOs often do not share their "profits" with their member hospitals. Moreover, member hospitals that do receive reimbursement do not always report this to Medicare, as the law requires. Meanwhile, the Justice Department is conducting a wide criminal investigation of Novation, the largest GPO, and many of its big supplier partners. Further, the Connecticut Attorney General has subpoenaed Healthcare Research and Development Institute (HRDI), a secretive organization made up of dominant suppliers and prominent hospital CEOs, and a number of its members in his investigation of possible "undue influence" by large vendors on hospital purchasing. And in February 2005, documents in the landmark Masimo vs. Tyco federal antitrust case, in which a Los Angeles jury awarded Masimo $420 million in actual and punitive damages, dispelled the notion that GPOs save hospitals money. Indeed, these documents show that the opposite is true. Once Masimo was able to sell its highly acclaimed pulse oximeters, which monitor patient oxygen levels, the price of these devices plunged by about 30%, demonstrating once again that competition, not cartels, drives down prices. Masimo was able to obtain contracts only because of the high profile it attained as poster child for the GPO issue. Most small companies haven't been as fortunate.

Now, it appears that we are approaching the endgame in the long struggle to eliminate one of the key obstacles to medical device innovation created by the purchasing cartels and the dominant manufacturers. For my company, which manufactures and markets VanishPoint® automated retraction safety needle devices, the struggle to gain access to America's private, acute care hospitals and protect their workers from potentially deadly accidental needlestick injuries has gone on for nearly a decade. Regrettably, the GPOs and their big manufacturer partners—Becton Dickinson in our case—are just as brazen in their illegal, anti-competitive conduct as they were on April 30, 2002, when you held your first hearing. We have evidence that Becton Dickinson, perhaps in an attempt to avoid further government scrutiny, and possibly with a wink and a nod from the big GPOs, is paying hefty upfront fees to big hospital systems to obtain long-term, exclusive contracts with these facilities. For example, a senior purchasing officer for the Pittsburgh-based West Penn Allegheny Health Systems bluntly told one of our salesmen, in effect, that BD had bought their business. So the big GPOs have essentially become the role models for a new generation of mini-GPOs that are dedicated to the principle that greed rules, and the patient and healthcare worker be damned.

So when I read the drafts of the three GPO reform bills now before this Subcommittee, I was elated to learn that you have agreed with our conclusion that there is too much at stake here, in the lives and health and well-being of America's patients and healthcare workers, not to mention money, to rely on the false promises and sham codes of conduct of the purchasing cartels to fix this critical healthcare problem. To be sure, this Subcommittee's insistence that the GPOs write and enforce voluntary codes of conduct was a useful and appropriate first step in addressing this problem, but this problem clearly requires a legislative fix. And in my opinion, the only legislative remedy that will solve this problem once and for all happens, not surprisingly, to be the simplest and shortest of the three legislative options on the table today: repeal of the Medicare/Medicaid anti-kickback safe harbor. Before elaborating on this, I'd like to put to rest (at the risk of beating a dead horse) the notion that the GPO industry is capable of policing itself with a code of conduct. I have reached this conclusion largely because of my own company's experience, but also because believing that the GPOs would abide by such a code simply defies logic. Their "pay to play" business model, in which the big vendors, not the hospitals, are their real customers, would be destroyed if they did so.

Back in April 2002, when you first pressed the GPOs to develop and implement a code of ethical conduct to address the abuses identified by this Subcommittee, I remained skeptical but was still willing to be pleasantly surprised. Unfortunately, three years later, nothing has changed. As I indicated in the statement I submitted for a previous hearing, our salespeople are no longer escorted to the parking lots of GPO member hospitals by security guards, but we are still blocked from marketing to the vast majority of these facilities. That is the case despite the fact that our automated retraction safety needle devices have been recognized by independent safety panels as the safest needle devices on the market today, and our pricing—on a per unit or all-in cost basis—is well below that of Becton Dickinson, the dominant manufacturer. In contrast to our experience with the GPO-controlled facilities, we continue to make significant progress in marketing our lifesaving devices to *public* facilities and agencies. In the U. S., our customers include the Centers for Disease Control, Veterans hospitals, the U. S. military, the New York City Fire Department and Department of Corrections. In Ohio and Wisconsin, respectively, they include Clark County Combined Health District and Clark County jail in Springfield and the Milwaukee County Mental Health Division and the Milwaukee County Jail, to name just a few. One of the most telling developments is the fact that in August we signed a licensing agreement with a Chinese medical device maker designated by China CDC to manufacture and distribute up to 400 million of our safety syringes annually in China. Ironically, free market competition in the medical device industry is alive and well in China, but moribund in the U. S. The repeal of the safe harbor would represent a major breakthrough in allowing us to compete here at home on the basis of quality, safety and cost-effectiveness, just like we are now able to do in China!

Moreover, we just received our second contract to supply our safety syringes under the President's Global HIV/AIDS initiative. We have received the largest contracts for safety syringes under this program. What that means is that the world's most advanced protection against needlestick injuries is now available to healthcare workers in some of the most impoverished countries in Africa and within two years will be widely available to workers in China. But because of the corrupt, anti-competitive GPO system in the U. S., this same protection is denied to workers in all but a handful of GPO-controlled private acute care hospitals here at home. That says it all.

As I indicated earlier, another reason the code of conduct cannot work is that it is diametrically at odds with the prevailing GPO business model in which big vendors pay huge fees to the GPOs to buy exclusive access to their member hospitals. The suppliers, not the hospitals, are their customers. Under this system, the GPOs have every incentive to demand ever-higher fees, and the big vendors have every incentive to pay them. Meanwhile, the hospitals have no incentives to save money, because the government will reimburse them for the higher costs. Under the current system, greed is king.

Indeed, there is no evidence that industry codes of conduct in general have ever amounted to more than PR spin. Codes of conduct written by the mining and defense industries are examples of codes than weren't worth the paper they were printed on. And this GPO code of conduct is no different.

With tens of billions of Medicare and Medicaid dollars at stake, Congress should not count on the GPOs to abide by a voluntary code of conduct—essentially an honor system—any more than the IRS should disband its anti-fraud units and ask taxpayers to promise that they won't cheat on their taxes.

In reviewing the drafts of the three bills now before this Subcommittee, it is clear to me, as it has been from the outset, that the repeal of the safe harbor represents the only viable and lasting solution to this problem. Our current predicament is yet another example of the law of unintended consequences. In enacting the ill-conceived anti-kickback safe harbor back in the 1980's, Congress may have had the best of intentions. But it did not foresee that these GPOs would soon divorce their financial interests from those of the hospitals and acquire enormous financial power for themselves. Over the last decade, the safe harbor has morphed, if you will, into a "pirate's cove" for monopolistic manufacturers with inferior products seeking to avoid the rigors of free and fair competition.

Repeal of the safe harbor would set the stage for the resurrection of the original, legitimate GPO business model, in which small hospitals banded together to obtain volume discounts from manufacturers. We have no quarrel whatsoever with that model, and never did.

Under this scenario, the GPOs would once again be accountable to—and be paid by—their real customers: America's hospitals. The beauty of this legislation lies in its simplicity. By reverting to the status quo ante, in which people who paid kickbacks faced the prospect of jail time, at least in theory, you would address and eradicate a multitude of sins.

Although the other two draft bills target many of the anti-competitive practices you have identified in your hearings, in my opinion they suffer to one degree or another from two distinct shortcomings.

First, they leave open the possibility—indeed the probability—that the GPOs and their big company partners will devise new and even more imaginative anti-competitive loopholes that circumvent the specific provisions of these bills. We have always given the devil his due. No one ever said the GPOs weren't clever.

Second, both of these bills would require an enormous regulatory apparatus to monitor compliance. The American healthcare system has already paid a steep price in human and financial terms for this corrupt system. Let's not raise the tab by creating another bloated, expensive bureaucracy just to keep the GPOs honest.

Let me conclude by saying that thanks to your leadership, we now find ourselves at a defining moment in the ongoing struggle to fix America's broken healthcare system. Repealing the anti-kickback safe harbor won't cure everything that ails this system. Indeed, in the early 1990's, some folks in Washington learned the hard way that there is no quick fix.

But repealing the safe harbor would go a long way towards enabling patients and providers to once again have the benefit of the best, safest, and most cost effective medical technology that American ingenuity can devise.

Repealing the safe harbor would remove one of the major tools used by the giant purchasing cartels and the monopolistic manufacturers to suppress free market competition in the American healthcare industry.

Repealing the safe harbor would help re-ignite the spark of innovation in the medical supply and device industry that has been virtually extinguished by nearly a decade of corrupt, anti-competitive practices.

And that would be no small accomplishment.

Thank you again for your deep concern and kind attention.

###

Testimony of

Dr. S. Prakash Sethi

University Distinguished Professor of Management and

President of the International Center for Corporate Accountability (ICCA), Zicklin

School of Business, Baruch College, the City University of New York

Before the

United States Senate

Committee on the Judiciary Subcommittee on

Antitrust, Competition Policy, and Consumer Rights *

Hearing on

"Hospital Group Purchasing:

Are the Industry's Reforms Sufficient to Ensure Competition?"

March 15, 2006

* The following members of ICCA's research staff contributed to the preparation of this testimony and the full report on GPOs and are greatly acknowledged: Ms. Olga Emelianova, Director for Project Services; Mr. Gianmarco Torterolo, Senior Research Analyst; Mr. Sandeep Hajare, Senior Research Analyst; Ms. Konstantina Kyrgidou, Research Analyst.

Mr. Chairman and Members of the Subcommittee:

Good afternoon. I wish to thank you for giving me the opportunity to appear as a witness today in my capacity as University Distinguished Professor of Management and President of the International Center for Corporate Accountability, Inc. (ICCA) at Baruch College of the City University of New York. I would also like to congratulate you on your thorough work on this complex and critical healthcare issue over the last several years and on your obvious determination to ensure free competition in the medical supply marketplace.

As I understand it, my assignment today is to examine the Healthcare Group Purchasing Industry Initiative ("GPO Initiative") and to offer my views on whether it will be sufficient to ensure competition in the healthcare supply industry. This topic has tremendous implications for the delivery of healthcare services in the United States, and I am pleased to be able to share my insights on this matter.

Let me begin by saying that I have spent a large part of my academic career of more than 30 years studying, analyzing, writing and implementing corporate and industry codes of conduct. I have published numerous articles and several books on this topic, most recently Setting Global Standards: Guidelines for Creating Codes of Conduct in Multinational Corporations, which was published in 2003.

At ICCA, a not-for-profit education-research organization based at Baruch, one of our main areas of research has been voluntary codes of conduct or principles, which are being created in increasingly large numbers by corporations and industry groups. We have undertaken numerous studies to analyze their substance and efficacy.

From 1984 to 1991, I worked closely with anti-apartheid groups and multinational corporations in implementing the Sullivan Principles in South Africa, which were aimed at promoting fair employment and eliminating apartheid. This was the most ambitious effort of its kind in my lifetime and involved over 150 U.S.-based multinational corporations. In my opinion, it also happens to be the only truly successful industry code of conduct ever implemented.

Industry-Based Codes of Conduct or Principles

Before looking specifically at the GPO Initiative, I'd like to offer an overview on industry codes of conduct and to discuss briefly the methodology we use at the ICCA for evaluating the substance and efficacy of codes of conduct.

Voluntary industry codes of conduct or principles can potentially play a critical role in engendering public trust in the conduct of an industry. A code of conduct is in the nature of a "private law" or a "promise voluntarily made" whereby an institution makes a public commitment to adhere to certain standards of conduct. The "private law" character of voluntary codes gives the sponsoring organizations a large measure of discretionary action. At the same time, it imposes on them the burden of ensuring that their critics and the public-at-large believe in the institutions' performance claims. In turn, if they are to accomplish that they almost invariably have to create independent systems of performance evaluation, monitoring and verification, and public disclosure.

Extensive studies by ICCA of a large number of industry-wide codes suggest that most of these codes have failed because of the unwillingness or inability of their sponsors to create and implement meaningful codes and standards. This is not surprising, since most industry-based initiatives are created in the aftermath of unethical and illegal activities on the part of the member companies

Industry members generally do not go beyond superficial statements of broad principles and a promise to make a good faith effort to improve their performance. Only a handful of industry codes, including those developed by the Forestry Council, electronics industry, and the toy industry, have had any impact at all on the conduct of their member companies. Conversely, oil and gas, mining and defense industries seem to have spent the most money to devise elaborate management and governance systems, but their codes have produced little improvement in the member companies' conduct. In my view, the GPO Initiative falls in the second category.

Based on our research and field work in monitoring code compliance, we have identified eight conditions that must be met for an industry-based code to demonstrate measurable and credible compliance with the industry's voluntary initiative.

1. The code must be substantive in addressing broad areas of public concern pertaining to industry's conduct.
2. Code principles or standards must be specific in addressing issues embodied in those principles.
3. Code performance standards must be realistic in the context of industry's financial strength and competitive environment. The industry should not make exaggerated promises or claim implausible achievements.
4. Member companies must create an effective internal implementation system to ensure effective code compliance.

5. Code compliance must be an integral part of a management performance evaluation and reward system.
6. The industry must create an independent governance structure that is not controlled by the executives of the member companies.
7. There must be an independent external monitoring and compliance verification system to engender public trust and credibility in the industry's claims of performance.
8. There should be maximum transparency and verifiable disclosure of industry performance to the public. Standards of performance disclosure should be the sole province of the code's governing board.

The GPO Initiative

With that as background, I'll now discuss the findings of our study of the GPO Industry Initiative. Over the last six months, my colleagues and I at ICCA have reviewed virtually all of the public record on the GPO issue, including Senate testimony, government and academic studies, legal proceedings, media reports, and relevant industry documents. We have evaluated the GPO Initiative against the principles I've just enumerated. For us, this is the customary process and a necessary precondition for drawing objective and unbiased conclusions.

From our analysis, it is apparent that GPOs play an extremely important role in the healthcare industry, one that is little understood by the general public and even many in the healthcare industry itself. The enormous size of the industry and the buying power they control would raise anti-competitive concerns under the best of circumstances -- that is, even if the marketplace were operating freely and openly. In the case of GPOs, the potential for abuse is even greater. Our detailed analysis of the public record, which is the basis for my comments, will be contained in a more comprehensive report by the ICCA to be submitted to the Subcommittee later.

This analysis strongly suggests that the current modus operandi of GPOs, doing business under the protection of the Medicare anti-kickback safe harbor, has contributed to a misallocation of a very large portion of the revenue received from vendors in the form of fees and other considerations. Like a spider's web, GPOs engulf both the buyers and suppliers in contractual arrangements that are questionable at best. This control allows them to engage in conduct that illegally and unethically enriches the GPOs at the expense of healthcare providers, new entrants, and the public-at-large. Regrettably, the failure of this industry to address these issues in the nearly four years -- since this panel first urged them to institute a code to police themselves -- continues the pattern of resistance to change that we have seen time and again with industry codes.

In my professional opinion, the current GPO business model and legal framework has built-in structural flaws, and its financial incentives are so perverse that the GPO Initiative cannot possibly remedy this situation. Anti-competitive contractual arrangements, industry concentration, and especially the vendor-financed fee structure--- all of which arise from the Medicare anti-kickback safe harbor -- have created strong incentives for the GPOs to maximize their income, and equally strong disincentives to distribute this income to their beneficial owners, i.e. hospitals and nursing homes. Indeed, the structure of the new GPO Initiative seems to indicate that its entire purpose is to protect the industry's anti-competitive, exclusionary system, in which the GPOs' self-interest takes precedence over the welfare of the industry's clients, including healthcare providers, taxpayers, and potential new entrants in the industry.

I do not believe that we can even begin to talk seriously about a GPO Initiative until we have realigned these financial incentives so that the hospitals, and not the vendors, are once again the GPOs' only clients. As long as vendors continue to pay fees to the GPOs, any attempt to create, implement and enforce a code of conduct is doomed to failure.

Creating a new competitive environment will require the repeal of the Medicare anti-kickback safe harbor provision. I might add parenthetically that this provision was a new one for me. As a patient, and as a New Yorker who thought he'd been around the block a few times, I was surprised to learn that there was an industry in this country in which the federal government has essentially continued to protect a system of monopolistic conduct long after the provision had lost any usefulness as an instrument of public policy to improve the economic efficiency of the healthcare delivery system.

Let's now look at the six principles contained in the GPO Initiative. Even a cursory reading of these principles would make it obvious that they urge the member companies to do things that they should have been doing in the first place without the need of a new set of principles. What is missing, and what is needed, is an honest recognition of the member companies' activities that have been found to be inappropriate.

I respectfully submit that an objective and thoughtful assessment would conclude that these principles fail to measure up, even at the very minimal level, against any of the eight criteria that I have just described. Among the most serious shortcomings of this Initiative are:

1. There is a total lack of independence in the Initiative's governance structure, which is entirely controlled by the top executives of the member companies. Although the Initiative includes a so-called "coordinator," the coordinator has no real authority.
2. Principles are essentially a statement of intent. Any description of what these principles might contain by way of substance is left entirely to the member companies.
3. Member companies also set their own criteria with regard to standards of compliance, performance evaluation, implementation assurance, and public disclosure. Reduced to its bare essentials, the final product of this process becomes nothing more than a compilation of the reports provided by the member companies based on their own self-evaluation.
4. The governance structure of the GPO Initiative does not provide any mechanism for independent external monitoring and verification of member companies' self-reported performance. Instead, it expects the public to accept this self-reported performance at face value. Such an assertion would be a dubious proposition under the best of circumstances. It would be untenable given the industry's current record.

Conclusion

In summary, the new GPO Initiative is encumbered with a lack of specificity, non-existent performance standards, an internally controlled and self-serving governance structure, and an absence of independent external monitoring system. It is unlikely to yield any meaningful reform. Instead it would exacerbate the problem through absence of meaningful change and would further erode the credibility of its sponsors.

It is unrealistic to expect an industry to create a viable code or initiative that has been operating with a business model based on perverse financial incentives, a questionable legal structure, and federal statutes that undermine the imperatives of competitive markets. Therefore, the repeal of the safe harbor must precede any discussion of a GPO industry code of conduct or initiative.

Restoration of market-based competition would be the first step to create a healthy business model for the entire healthcare industry. While market competition can go a long way in minimizing illegal and unethical practices, it cannot completely eliminate them. This is where industry-wide codes of conduct can potentially play an important role in narrowing the gap between societal expectations and industry performance.

After Congress acts to restore market competition to this industry, I would recommend that the healthcare industry develop a code of conduct that encourages a higher level of ethical and legal conduct. Such a code would adhere to the above mentioned eight criteria for creating and implementing effective codes of conduct. I would urge that such a code not be limited to the GPOs but also include the other two groups in this equation. These are: (i) healthcare providers, i.e., hospitals and nursing homes; and, (ii) the suppliers of medical products and services. As I indicated earlier, a voluntary industry-based code faces an uphill battle under the best of circumstances and cannot possibly succeed unless all parties act in good faith and are truly committed to its success. I earnestly hope that these conditions would emerge once competition has been restored to the healthcare supply industry. This would provide a rare opportunity for the industry leaders, i.e., executives of hospitals, GPOs, and suppliers, to take the lead by creating a truly meaningful code of conduct that would be the role model for other industries.

Thank you for your attention. I would be pleased to try to answer any questions.

Date: March 15, 2006

Comments on the Proposed "Ensuring Competition in Hospital Purchasing Act"

S. Prakash Sethi, Ph.D.

In my view, enacting this bill is the most significant and far reaching action that the U.S. Senate-Congress can take to bring greater efficiency, reduced costs, and increased transparency in an opaque area of costs-benefits related to the operations of GPOs, hospitals, nursing homes, and other healthcare providers.

Because of the enormous amount of money involved even a small reduction in GPO costs can yield substantial benefits to the hospitals, nursing homes and other healthcare providers that are covered by GPO-contracted and managed purchasing programs.

For obvious reasons, GPOs are adamantly opposed to the elimination of safe harbor provisions. In defending their role and justifying their modus operandi, GPOs make a variety of unsubstantiated and unverifiable assertions concerning the savings they achieve and pass on to their beneficial owners, i.e., hospitals, nursing homes and other healthcare providers. They also make claims for their economic efficiencies in negotiating lower prices from their suppliers, which are passed on to the GPOs' beneficial owners. Thirdly, they raise the specter of hospitals being deprived of savings and surpluses distributed by the GPOs in the event that the safe harbor is repealed and the administrative fee is phased out. It is alleged that these hospitals are struggling from higher costs and thus need all the extra savings that GPOs can provide them. The impression, invariably created but never supported with data and facts by GPOs, is that the repeal of safe harbor would amount to financial catastrophe for a large number of hospitals, nursing homes, and other healthcare providers.

There is no question as to the desirability of hospitals, nursing homes and other healthcare providers to combine their purchases and thereby leverage their buying power to negotiate lower prices and volume discounts. However, the benefits of combined purchases are greatly reduced under conditions where the middleman, i.e., GPOs, control the entire process through restrictive arrangements with suppliers and customers. These arrangements allow them to capture a large portion of the gains from group purchasing activities. These excessive agency costs, i.e., compensation for the GPOs, are further facilitated through GPOs' control of all relevant financial information; and, where the governance and accountability structure of these activities is largely, if not entirely, controlled by the GPO management. To the extent that GPOs are profit-making organizations – or largely self-governing because of weak oversight on the part of hospitals and other healthcare providers - the current arrangement provides GPOs with the most opportunity and also the maximum incentive to structure their operations in a manner that would maximize their income and management rewards at the expense of those who should be the ultimate beneficiaries of the program, i.e., hospitals, nursing homes and other healthcare providers. Under these circumstances, seeking lower prices from the suppliers take a back seat to higher returns generated by products that maximize revenue for GPOs through administrative fee payments.

It is also contestable that the large size of GPOs, through consolidation, yield further economies of scale as alleged by the GPOs to be self-evident. If this were the case, large organizations would almost always be more efficient than small and medium size organizations. We should then need only one GPO to serve the entire industry. Under this assertion, one would expect the recent consolidation of GPOs to deliver lower overall and per capita operational costs by the three GPOs, which together control approximately 75% market share of all GPO-contracted and managed purchases. Available data, however, indicate otherwise. Rather than declining, overall operating costs as claimed by these GPOs have increased with every enlargement in their size.

Experience in the competitive marketplace provides substantial evidence to indicate that small and medium size organizations often can be more effective and flexible in their operations and in their response to market conditions. Transaction cost economics theory suggests that all transactions have certain costs attached to them and that beyond a certain size these costs increase in larger organizations because of their increased complexity, bureaucratic controls, and multiple layers of management. Therefore, it is important to separate large size of the organization from large number of transactions to ascertain the relative efficiency of size to transaction costs.

The 3% Administrative Fee

One of the most egregious and utterly false arguments made by GPOs is that the loss of 3% administrative fee, currently protected under the safe harbor, would have crippling effect on the ability of the hospitals, nursing homes and other healthcare providers, to sustain their group buying activities. Furthermore, these institutions would also lose their share of the surpluses created through the administrative fee and distributed by GPOs to their member hospitals.

It should be apparent to everyone that GPOs' current suppliers are not running a charity and that any fee that they have to pay, no matter what it is called, eventually would have to be added to their costs and reflected in the prices they charge for their products. When this fee is eliminated, the money saved does not evaporate in thin air. It would either be reflected in lower prices charged by the suppliers, or someone else would have windfall profits.

The current system of administrative fee has no relation whatsoever to the cost of running GPO operations. Nor is it related to the efficiency and cost of products contracted by different suppliers. Instead, it has become a system of "pay to play" where the middlemen, i.e., GPOs, attempt to maximize their revenue by increasing the total size of purchases. And, all other things being equal, a higher priced product would yield a higher level of revenue to the middleman.

Evidence of this type of self-enrichment and conflict of interest can be seen through instances of side deals, supplier provided compensation to GPO managers above and beyond the 3% fee and not reported or shared with the member hospitals, and creation of captive suppliers. These and other examples of GPO conduct have been revealed through federal investigations and private lawsuits. It should also be noted that Connecticut's Attorney General has initiated another investigation with regard to GPO activities as reported by the Attorney General in his written testimony to the Senate Judiciary Committee's hearing of March 15, 2006.

For the GPOs, if a contract in year one requires an administrative fee of 3%, the same contract should need a lower administrative fee in the following year because the volume has gone up and the negotiating costs have gone down. While the total cost of managing larger volumes may go up, the unit cost of managing a larger volume of supplies should go down. Higher volumes under the same old contract do not increase GPOs' operating costs by the same amount and should in fact reduce the administrative fee/cost per unit. Therefore, GPOs stand to make more money from their 3% fee because their administrative costs would go down. Conversely, they could indicate that they have become more efficient and thus pay their managers larger performance bonuses.

From the viewpoint of the suppliers, it is in their interest to have the longest possible production run of a product even when it is outmoded because they do not have to incur additional costs of machines and tooling. By the same token, if their costs go down because of economies of scale, and also because capital costs have been depreciated, they would make increasingly more money from older products than from newer products even when they continue to pay the same 3% administrative fee.

Under this arrangement, everybody comes out ahead except the hospitals that use these products. This is so because the hospitals invariably get older products and do not receive the benefit of lower prices or greater savings from the administrative fee. Although, the situation has not been thoroughly investigated, available evidence from GAO and other investigative reports suggests that GPOs do not always secure lower prices or best products. GPOs' operating costs also have not been analyzed to assess their efficiency and reasonabless.

There are three problems with the fixed fee arrangement, which cause them to lose any direct and meaningful relationship to the cost of service that this fee is intended to cover. One, instead of creating incentives toward lower costs and better efficiencies, a constant fee rate creates incentives that do the opposite, i.e., while the actual costs may be going down, the prices paid remain constant to eliminate the possibility of earning lower revenue from the administrative fee by the GPOs. Two, the fee structure generates rewards that further retard the process of innovation and cost efficiencies. Three, the most important thing for the hospitals and policymakers to understand is that the administrative fee is not some "free good" delivered by the suppliers out of the goodness of their heart. For them, it is just another cost of doing business. Someone must pay this cost and it is reflected in the price at which these goods are sold by the suppliers.

Transition Phase

Repeal of safe harbor and its administrative fee structure would necessarily involve disruption in established business practices and current contractual relationships between the suppliers, GPOs and their beneficial owners. Therefore, a transition period and some short-term facilitating arrangements would be necessary.

1. An important first step would be to separate from the GPOs, the control and management of funds generated from the administrative fee from the GPOs. The current situation is structurally flawed and creates conflict of interest. This system is akin to a situation where SEC or IRS are responsible for collecting money for the government. However, instead of turning this money over to the Treasury Department, they assume the authority for deciding as to how much money they should hold for their own use, and how the remainder should be allocated to other government departments and Federal agencies.

2. Hospitals and other healthcare providers should have complete freedom to buy products from their suppliers or other competitors where lower costs, better service, or improved products are available. Furthermore, GPOs should have no control over the decisions made by the hospitals and other healthcare providers, who are members of a particular GPO.

3. GPOs must not control the process of scientific evaluation of new products. There is an inherent conflict of interest as GPOs have a vested interest to protect their revenue flows from current suppliers. The scientific evaluation committees should be established by the hospitals, in consultation with the medical community. The decisions of these committees should be transparent and made public. In case a GPO disagrees with this decision, the burden of proof must be placed on the GPO and subject to override by an independent body comprised of representatives of the member hospitals, nursing homes and other healthcare providers.

In the long term, competitive markets would create various alternatives for covering the administrative costs associated with group buying programs in a manner that would balance the interests of both the suppliers and their customers. A market-based system would clearly be superior to the current arrangement. It would also obviate the necessity of cumbersome regulatory mechanisms, which are susceptible to manipulation through "technicalities," excessive delays, and political influence on the part of GPOs and other parties who stand to benefit from a protected business environment.

Comments on S.2880 "Medical Device Competition Act 2004" (Introduced in Senate) 108th Congress, 2nd Session

S. Prakash Sethi, Ph.D.

I have a number of serious problems with this proposed bill:

First, the regulatory enforcement of this bill would be highly adversarial. The organizations to be regulated, i.e., GPOs would have a strong financial incentive to prolong and even scuttle all enforcement efforts because every delay and dilution translates into substantial financial gains.

Second, an adversarial regulatory environment would require substantial commitment of financial and professional resources on the part of the regulatory authorities. S.2880 does not require the Department of Health and Human Services to make any such commitments. Therefore, implementation of these regulations would be highly vulnerable to the changing priorities of the Department of Health and Human Services, as well as the changing political climate in the Congress. Thus while the GPOs current practices will continue, their effective regulation is not necessarily ensured even with the passage of this S.2880.

Third, the current effort at regulating GPOs is vulnerable to unequal financial, political, and organizational leverage. GPOs, who are the primary beneficiaries of the status quo, are a highly focused, amply financed, and well-organized group. It could and certainly would mobilize significant financial resources to dilute and delay effective enforcement of S.2880. If this bill is enacted into law in 2006, GPOs would have two years to continue business as usual and also devise other ways, which would allow them to maintain their strong hold on the purchasing process, without violating this law. Moreover these groups have the will and the means to persist in their efforts over a long period of time.

Conversely, the groups that stand to gain from a strong and effective regulatory oversight are widely dispersed and poorly organized. They include, among others, hospitals, nursing homes, other healthcare providers, the vast patient population and ultimately the American public. In their current mode, they lack adequate financial and informational resources, effective organizational mechanisms, and political muscle with which to counterbalance the potential power and influence of GPOs.

Another problem with S.2880 is that it is non-specific as to what constitutes "reasonable costs." This is necessarily left to future rule-making by the Department of Health and Human Services. The regulatory history of the Federal Trade Commission, Consumer Safety Commission and other similar bodies, is replete with instances where larger companies would dump truckloads of documents asserting that this information supported the companies' position while fully knowing that FTC did not have the resources to evaluate and analyze those documents. This situation invariably leads to a settlement in terms that are at best face-saving on the part of the regulators without necessarily bringing about significant changes in the conduct of the companies' conduct.

Adequate enforcement requires sufficient staff and financial resources, which are not always available given our history of budget tightening in the arena of health and human services. Hence, there would always be pressure to cut back in one area in order to meet other "more important" priorities. It should be apparent that GPOs would have every incentive in the world to overplay the "so-called unnecessary cost" of this regulation.

Based on my analysis, I respectfully submit that S.2880 is unlikely to change the current competitive environment and operational practices of the GPOs. While I could make a number of suggestions for improving S.2880, I believe that the more viable approach is to eliminate the fundamental agency/stewardship conflict that gave rise to the questionable GPO practices in the first place, that can only be accomplished, in my opinion, by repealing the anti-kickback safe harbor.

Comments on the Proposed

"Hospital Group Purchasing Organization Reform Act"

By S. Prakash Sethi, Ph.D.

In my opinion, the proposed legislation is inadequate for the task assigned to it and is unlikely to be effective without important changes in its scope and the manner of its operation. This proposed Act provides only a broad framework for creating an industry-based code and leaves the entire process of code creation, implementation, monitoring, and compliance assurance, entirely to "self-regulation" on the part of the GPOs. This is a dangerous proposition given the fact that GPOs are adamantly opposed to a code of conduct that goes beyond generalities as to standards of performance and does not have meaningful assurance of compliance with code standards, however, ambiguous and superficial. In the absence of compliance standards that are outcome oriented and not merely process oriented; and, a compliance verification system that is independently monitored and certified, the proposed Act would fail to achieve any of its intended objectives. Instead, it would result in negating any potential benefits that might come from the establishment of the Hospital Group Purchasing Organizations Ethics and Business Practices Compliance Office and its certification of GPOs.

The conditions outlined in the Act as to the GPO code of conduct are entirely process oriented and do not mention any requirements for creating standards that would specify minimum levels of compliance, activities that would be strictly proscribed, a requirement that a GPO would be legally liable and subject to civil and even criminal penalties, for making false and inaccurate claims as to its performance under the code.

To be effective an industry code of conduct must also have a governance process that is independent of the GPOs whose activities it is supposed to monitor and verify. It would also be beneficial to separate the primary activities of GPOs, i.e., negotiate and manage group purchasing contracts with suppliers, from the role of collecting and disbursing the proceeds of administrative fee received from the suppliers.

An industry code of conduct must have important representation in its governance and oversight structure from the beneficiaries of the group purchasing system, and in whose sole interest the GPOs are supposed to operate. These are the hospitals, nursing homes, and other healthcare providers whose purchases are being facilitated by the GPOs. Otherwise, the code content and its implementation would be reduced to the self-serving claims by the GPOs. An effective measure to overcome this situation would be to treat the official reports by the GPOs as "implied contract" and thus any false claims made in these reports would be subject to legal proceedings and penalties. The new Act should specifically allow private action by injured parties against GPOs where GPOs self-evaluation reports of compliance with the industry's code of conduct would be considered as a factual statement of the GPOs activities.

International Center for Corporate Accountability, Inc.

Ensuring Integrity, Accountability & Transparency in Business Worldwide

April 18, 2006

The Honorable Mike DeWine
United States Senate
Committee on the Judiciary
Washington, DC 20510-6275

Dear Senator DeWine:

I had the privilege of testifying before your Subcommittee on Antitrust, Competition, Policy, and Consumer Rights at the hearing entitled, "Hospital Group Purchasing: Are the Industry's Reform Sufficient to Ensure Competition?" on March 15, 2006. I respectfully request that the Committee records should indicate that I testified in my personal capacity and that the views expressed by me at the hearing are not to be attributed to Baruch College or the International Center for Corporate Accountability, Inc.

Thank you.

Sincerely,

Prof. S. Prakash Sethi
University Distinguished Professor
President

cc: Mr. Seth Bloom
Mr. Douglas Rathburn

Zicklin School of Business Baruch College CUNY 1 Bernard Baruch Way, J1034, New York, NY 10010
tel.: (646) 312-2230 fax: (646) 312-2231 www.ICCA-corporateaccountability.org

SUBCOMMITTEE ON ANTITRUST, COMPETITION POLICY AND CONSUMER RIGHTS, COMMITTEE ON THE JUDICIARY UNITED STATES SENATE

TESTIMONY OF MINA UBBING

President and CEO, Fairfield Medical Center
Lancaster, Ohio

March 15, 2006

Good afternoon. My name is Mina Ubbing, President and CEO of Fairfield Medical Center in Lancaster, Ohio. I'd like to thank Chairman DeWine and Ranking Member Kohl for inviting me to testify today before the Subcommittee on Antitrust, Competition Policy and Consumer Rights. It's a special pleasure to be here before a fellow Ohioan, Chairman DeWine.

Background

I appreciate the opportunity to speak about the way in which the health care supply chain operates, having spent 27 years in the field of healthcare finance. In 2001, I was appointed President and CEO of Fairfield Medical Center, and before that served as Fairfield's CFO. I began my career as an auditor and hospital controller, and have spent the subsequent years entrenched in the finances of Ohio health care systems. I have also taught health care purchasing management at the college level.

Fairfield Medical Center is a 222-bed, not-for-profit, general acute care facility. Established in 1916, our community hospital has grown to become a widely respected, modern system and a major referral center serving the healthcare needs of southeastern Ohio region. I am extremely proud that Fairfield has twice been named the Lancaster Fairfield County

Chamber of Commerce Business of the Year, and a finalist for HealthLeaders' Top Leadership Teams in Healthcare last year. We were also one of 21 hospitals in the nation to be recognized for our recycling and environmental awareness efforts.

I bring to this hearing my perspective not only as FMC's CEO, but additionally as the chair of the Ohio Valley Hospital Consortium, a four-hospital regional collaborative entity. I have also served for nearly 2 years on the Board of the Ohio Hospital Association, and in that sense I believe I speak for all the 170 hospitals who are members of that organization.

The Health Care Purchasing Marketplace

As the members of this subcommittee are undoubtedly aware, America's health care systems are under tremendous pressure to deliver health care at affordable prices, and to do so without undermining the financial well-being of our own delivery systems. In addition to providing top flight health care professionals, we must maintain an inventory of goods and services that enable us to provide the highest quality of care to every surgical patient, every emergency room visitor, every expectant mother, and every individual in need of medical testing.

Doing this requires us not simply to stockpile bandages and bedpans. Rather, in today's environment -- in which costs continue to increase while fees are held flat and federal reimbursements steadily decline – hospital purchasing extends from pharmaceutical compounds to food service, from syringes to state of the art imaging systems. We must bear the cost of infrastructure improvements as much as the cost of constantly upgrading and replacing our equipment, and we must do it all on a very tight budget.

The Value of GPO Membership

At Fairfield Medical Center, we purchase thousands of categories of goods and services, and have relationships with more than 1,600 vendors. Every day, our materials manager has to put tens of thousands of items in our hospital; our pharmacy has an equally large burden. And while ours is a strong and well-respected hospital, we are relatively small and our power in the enormous health care purchasing marketplace is modest.

That is why we have long been a member of a health care group purchasing organization, or "GPO." For more than 22 years, FMC has been a proud member of Amerinet, and we have reaped tremendous benefits from that relationship by being able to leverage Amerinet's market expertise and market power.

The hard dollar savings to FMC directly attributable to participating in Amerinet are roughly $1.1 million per year. These savings do not reflect the many other values that we get from being part of Amerinet, including education, assistance in negotiating for non-Amerinet products, and benchmarking of FMC's performance against our peers. If FMC were forced to perform its own contracting in place of those GPO services we use, we would need to add at least 5 new professional staff positions to our purchasing department, at an annual cost of at least $400,000. And without the nationwide knowledge of products and prices currently maintained by our GPO, FMC would be at a further disadvantage in negotiating our own contracts, likely yielding even more erosion of our pricing power. I need hardly tell you that we simply cannot afford such a proposition.

FMC is fully aware of that Amerinet receives administrative fees from vendors and that these fees result from purchases that we and other Amerinet members make under our GPO contracts. Amerinet has always been extremely transparent with us and other members in terms of revenues they receive and services they provide. I believe these fees are quite reasonable, particularly measured against the benefits we receive from being part of a GPO – and against the value of the GPO to the suppliers themselves, who rely on GPOs to provide marketing and distribution support in exchange for the fees they pay.

Purchasing Decisions

That is not to say, of course, that we do all our purchasing through Amerinet. To the contrary, only about 63 percent of FMC's purchasing occurs through our GPO. Indeed, of the top 500 items purchased by FMC, only about half come from our GPO. The remainder we buy directly from vendors. FMC does not purchase sutures through Amerinet, for example, because Amerinet does not offer the brand that our clinicians demand. As such, we buy sutures direct from another manufacturer. This underscores a critical facet of hospital purchasing – namely, that hospitals do not make their purchasing decisions based only on what our GPOs have to offer. Purchasing decisions are driven by a variety of factors, including clinician preferences, our own comfort level with certain products and services; and the knowledge that our purchase is cost-effective, not just low-cost.

In other cases, we can access certain goods and services – items we buy locally, for instance – at already-low costs on our own. More often, however, we may wish to buy goods or services that our GPO does not offer on contract. In those cases, we go outside our GPO and make those purchases directly from the product vendor.

In the end, like all health care systems, FMC retains total control over its selection of products and technologies in use within the system. The portfolio offered by our GPO is a valued source of options, but any final decision about whether to use a GPO vendor or non-GPO vendor rests totally with us, and is driven by the types internal factors I have noted.

Indeed, when we consider whether to purchase a new device or innovative technology, we rely on a wide array of resources to guide our decision. We may seek input from clinicians, outside experts, manufacturers, government agencies, consulting firms and our GPO each time we contemplate acquiring something new. At FMC, we have established a Value Analysis Committee for all new medical technologies. Whether the technology comes to us at the request of a physician, through a trade show, through the recommendation of an outside consultant, or through a direct appeal from the potential vendor, we subject the proposed purchase to a 16-point "Value Inspection," an analysis we perform ourselves to measure the value of the product and its ability to meet clinical needs cost-effectively. A copy of our Value Inspection is attached hereto.

Ultimately, after we consider all these factors, the purchasing decision remains that of our hospital and our clinicians. There isn't a GPO in the nation that can dictate what we buy, or whether can get access to a medical technology that our clinicians believe is beneficial and needed in our system. If we need it, or if our clinical staff demands it, we purchase it. It's as simple as that.

One example of an item that our clinical staff required that we did not purchase through our GPO is a technology produced by a small Dublin, Ohio company called Neoprobe. Neoprobe makes a gamma detection device used in cancer surgery. When we could not buy this item through our GPO, we went directly to Neoprobe and established a vendor relationship.

Sometimes, moreover, items cannot be accessed through our GPO because the manufacturer will not sell on a GPO contract. This is often the case with items still under patent. In such cases, where the market has deemed the device to be a legitimate new innovation, we also buy directly from the vendor. One instance of this is with a California company called Kyphon, which produces an injectable substance for treatment of spinal pain. Kyphon does not sell this device through GPOs, and yet we purchase more of this product, measured in total spend, than any other surgical item in our hospital.

Restrictions on GPOs are a Direct Threat to Hospitals

The technological needs of FMC, like any health care system, are constantly changing. We can count on health care consumers to demand access to the best new technologies, just as our clinicians demand use of the same. We must be able to respond to these demands. That is why we have a system in place at FMC to identify and evaluate new medical technologies, and to acquire them when doing so is the right clinical and financial decision for our hospital.

In this light, GPOs do provide immense value to FMC and other health care systems, even though they hardly control our purchasing decisions. The GPO model of charging administrative fees to suppliers, and providing cost savings and other important benefits to FMC and other members, is critical for any health care system in today's economically challenging environment. This is particularly the case for small and rural systems like ours, which have the least market power and the most to lose from margin pressures.

If GPO administrative fees were eliminated and FMC had to pay its GPO as part of its operating expenses, we would realize an enormous net loss. I have little doubt that, wherever possible, we would have to look to shift the expense to health care consumers beyond governmental payors whose reimbursement rates are constantly being challenged From what I understand, it was this very threat that prompted Congress to establish the 'safe harbor' to Medicare rules that allows GPOs to operate as they currently do. Elimination of administrative fees would also, I expect, mean that our GPO would have to reduce or eliminate many of the other services that they provide to us.

Over the nearly three decades I have been a hospital administrator, I have seen many unintended consequences of well-intentioned but misguided efforts to better "control" business practices in the health care sector. Where GPOs are concerned, I believe that any restrictive legislation would have a dangerous and severe ripple effect on America's hospitals – adverse consequences that would be felt most severely by small and rural systems such as ours. There is no doubt in my mind that a voluntary initiative among the leaders of the GPO industry, like the one that General Bednar is here to describe, is the best available way to sustain ethical and transparent business practices among GPOs while preserving the savings and benefits that GPOs offer to us, and to patients who rely on us for excellent care.

We were made aware of the GPO Industry Initiative last year when the effort was launched by Amerinet and eight other leading GPOs. We are proud of what Amerinet and its colleagues in the GPO industry have done to form the Industry Initiative, and we believe that the Initiative sets a standard of industry practices by which all GPOs are judged. We have no interest in doing business with any GPO that is not willing to measure itself against the Industry Initiative's standards of conduct, and I suspect that most, if not all, other hospital CEOs feel the same way.

Mr. Chairman, Senator Kohl, members of the Subcommittee, I ask you to join me in recognizing the value that GPOs bring to the health care marketplace – to recognize that, while important, these entities do not control the purchasing marketplace, but rather help to make it a more robust, competitive, cost-effective and informed decision-making environment – and to support the continuation of the GPO Industry Initiative rather than any proposed legislation that would impose costly new restrictions on GPOs and the health care systems that depend on them.

Thank you for your consideration of my views.

Fairfield
Medical Center

Value Analysis Committee Meeting

March 8, 2006

Value Statement

- The Value Analysis Committee (VAC) will review the function of a product/technology, process, or a project using a standard format that measures the value of products and work process design to meet customers' needs at lowest possible total cost.

Committee Members

Radiology Gene Klinger	Nursing 6th South Becky Altier	Nursing Dept Pam Reed	Nursing PCU Debbie Tinto
Cardiac Cath Lab Kelly Fusselman	Safety Officer Isabelle Johns	Surgery Pavilion Sara Johnson	Surgery Pavilion Nancy McGushin
Laboratory Melissa O'Neal	Surgery Celeste Schmelzer	Infectious Disease Dr Andy Murry	Nursing ICU Nancy Stone
Materials Clinical Marilyn Wagner	Nursing- 4th Floor Tina Ward	Pharmacy Betsy Winsley	Business Office Sharon Scruggs
Materials- Distrib Sandra Clark	Purchasing Chuck Davis	Purchasing Tonya Julian	Purchasing Donna Roark

Ad Hoc Value Analysis Participants

Central Sterile	Infection Control	Nursing Supervisor
OB/Gyn	Biomed	ED
Physicians	Administration	Off-Sites
Staff Development	Environmental Svcs	Systems

Value Analysis Committee
What Our Customers Want

Include physicians and/or Medical Director	Establish Time frame for projects	User Friendly Paper Work	Clear and Understandable Policy
Understand when products cross multiple departments	Communicate in Monday Morning to include Physicians	Education to staff and Physicians	Clear delineation of what needs VAC process
Communicate to all departments when product is approved	Timely feedback	Limit the number of vendors per product for trial	Communicate, Communicate and Communicate

What The Committee Should Review

Products used facility wide or with the possibility of expanding from dept. to dept.	New technology for FMC with new products and equipment	Cost benefit/comparison High usage High cost Contract in/out	Housewide equipment: IV pumps Thermometers

Projects 2006

Infection Control	Diagnostic and Interventional	Safety	Critical Care	Patient Care
Equipment Sanitation-Sani-Wipes	*Closure Devices*	Sharps Safety-Safety Scalpels	*Pleurex Catheter Drainage System*	IV Pumps Administration
Percutaneous Devices-PICC CVP	Contrast Media	Protective Gear-Surgical and Exam Gloves	*Enteral Feeding*	Compression Devices-Bluflex
Urinary Drainage		Patient Apparel-Linens Textiles and Slippers	ResQPod Circulator Enhancer	Hypo/Hyperthermia Units
Blood Pressure Cuffs			*Cable Anchoring Device*	

Preparing for Value Analysis

- FDA searches-Maude reports-recall and alerts through ECRI
- Clinical Evidence-independent studies
- Other Users-contacting area users
- Cost Benefit Analysis- analytical data
- SKU Analysis- what other products are used for similar purpose
- Reimbursement Analysis

16 Point Value Inspection

Product Safety FDA Approved? FDA Recalls? FDA Safety Alerts or under investigation?	**Clinical Evidence** Is there clinical evidence to support the product claims?	**Reimbursement** Can FMC bill for and seek reimbursement for the cost of the product from 3rd Party Payers?	**Widely Accepted** Do other area hospitals use the product? Are their experiences favorable? Interdepartmental- will other departments be impacted with use?
Standardization Is this product standardized with the service line for cost reduction and improved efficiency?	**SKU's** What other SKU's provide the same function?	**Length of Stay-** Will the product use result in reduction in length of stay?	**Pain** Will the product significantly reduce the amount of pain experienced by patient?
Staff Efficiency Will the product improve efficiency in throughput, time, staff satisfaction?	**Physician Preference** Will the preference suit the needs of multiple clinicians and physicians?	**Vendor** Is the product available through a reputable supplier with whom FMC has an account?	**Sample Products** Will the supplier provide no charge samples for product trial?
Outcomes What problem does this product solve; what alternatives if not used or introduced?	**Cost Effective** Is the cost prohibitive and are there alternatives?	**Proprietary** Is the product the only one available for this specific use?	**Education** What is the level of training required to use this product?

Project Updates
Infection Control

- Equipment Sanitation- Sani-Wipes- completed 02/06; Intended uses
- Percutaneous Devices- reduction in SKUs- deferred to Dr Roche- meeting delays
- Urologicals- standardization to Bard products- conversion in process
- Blood Pressure Cuffs- bacteria colonization with reuseable cuffs- discuss next steps

Diagnostic and Interventional

- Femoral Closure Devices SafeGuard Assist and Boomerang- requests from Cath Lab; E-MUSIC information
- Contrast Media- standardization project results of evaluation from MRI

Safety Devices

- Scalpel- safety scalpel trial results

New Requests 2006

- Protective Apparel- gloves, gear
- Linens- patient linens and slippers

Critical Care

- ResQPod Circulator Enhancer

  New Requests for 2006

- *Pleurex Catheter Drainage System*
- *Enteral Feeding*
- *Cable Anchoring Device*

Patient Equipment

- IV Administration- update from subgroup

New Requests 2006

- Compression Devices
- Hypothermia Units